ORTHO'S All About

Landscape
Plans

Written and photographed by
Chuck Crandall and Barbara Crandall

Meredith® Books
Des Moines, Iowa

Ortho® Books
An imprint of Meredith® Books

Landscape Plans
Editor: Michael McKinley
Art Director: Tom Wegner
Copy Chief: Catherine Hamrick
Copy and Production Editor: Terri Fredrickson
Contributing Editor: Jo Kellum
Contributing Copy Editor: Roberta J. Peterson
Technical Proofreader: Mary Pas
Contributing Proofreaders: Kathy Eastman, Debra Morris
    Smith, Margaret Smith
Contributing Illustrators: Mike Eagleton, Tom Rosborough
Contributing Map Illustrator: Jana Fothergill
Indexer: Colleen Johnson
Electronic Production Coordinator: Paula Forest
Editorial and Design Assistants: Kathleen Stevens,
    Karen Schirm
Production Director: Douglas M. Johnston
Production Manager: Pam Kvitne
Assistant Prepress Manager: Marjorie J. Schenkelberg

**Additional Editorial Contributions from
    Art Rep Services**
Director: Chip Nadeau
Designer: Laura Rades

Meredith® Books
Editor in Chief: James D. Blume
Design Director: Matt Strelecki
Managing Editor: Gregory H. Kayko
Executive Ortho Editor: Benjamin W. Allen

Director, Sales & Marketing, Retail: Michael A. Peterson
Director, Sales & Marketing, Special Markets:
    Rita McMullen
Director, Sales & Marketing, Home & Garden Center
    Channel: Ray Wolf
Director, Operations: George A. Susral

Vice President, General Manager: Jamie L. Martin

Meredith Publishing Group
President, Publishing Group: Christopher M. Little
Vice President, Consumer Marketing & Development:
    Hal Oringer

Meredith Corporation
Chairman and Chief Executive Officer: William T. Kerr

Chairman of the Executive Committee: E.T. Meredith III

Cover photograph by Jerry Howard/Positive Images

All of us at Ortho® Books are dedicated to providing you
with the information and ideas you need to enhance your
home and garden. We welcome your comments and
suggestions about this book. Write to us at:
    Meredith Corporation
    Ortho Books
    1716 Locust St.
    Des Moines, IA 50309–3023

Thanks to
Melissa George, Aimee Reiman

Photography Credits:
All photographs except cover are by Crandall and Crandall.
    Landscape designers for the photographs are as follows
    (L= Left, R= Right, C= Center, B= Bottom, T= Top):
Jim and Mary McIntire: 4T, 12 Row 2-1
Hugh Dargan & Associates: 4C
Mario Mathias: 4B
Paradise Gardens: 5TL
Rogers Gardens: 5TR, 12 Row 2-4
John Herbst, Jr. & Associates: 5CR, 13 Row 1-4
Michael Glassman & Associates: 5BL, 12 Row 1-1, 12 Row
    1-3, 13 Row 3-1, 13 Row 3-2,
Cathy Morehead & Associates: 8C
Alice Menard: 8B
Ivy's Gardens: 9T
Gregg and Pam Bunch: 12 Row 1-2
Marianne Morse: 13 TR
Lani Berrington & Associates: 13 Row 1-2
Nick Williams & Associates: 13 Row 2-1, 13 Row 3-3

4

CREATING YOUR PERFECT LANDSCAPE

Creating your perfect landscape means adding your personal touch, whether you love riots of blooming color or a peaceful destination tucked deep in the garden.

Good planning results in a good landscape, whether you want a formal space, such as this colonial garden (left), or an informal, naturalized design.

How do you want to use your landscape? Planning begins with asking questions to determine your needs. Some landscape plans emphasize space for entertaining, others for play; this peaceful garden (right) promotes relaxation and tranquility.

A handsome, well-designed landscape is a universal goal among homeowners. From new houses in the suburbs to older homes in the city, only rarely do lucky homebuyers inherit the perfect garden from a previous owner. It usually takes some effort to create a yard that has all the features you want to make your landscape a joyful destination. Adding a personal touch claims outside space as an extension of your home.

If you have never designed a new landscape or remodeled an old one, the task of accomplishing your dreams may seem daunting. There's a lot to consider: How do you and your family want to use your landscape? How can you improve the front garden to create more curb appeal? Where's the best spot for the kids' play area? Asking yourself such questions is the beginning of the design process; determining what you need is the first step toward planning improvements.

In this book you will find 28 typical landscapes designed by 28 of the leading designers in the United States and Canada. Chances are, there's a plan for a site similar to yours. The variety of problems and solutions presented gives you the opportunity to find ideas you can adapt to your own property and its needs. Start by finding a plan that is characteristic of the configuration and terrain of your property. Study it carefully to find ideas you can use for your own landscape. But don't ignore plans for properties different from your own; you'll find plenty of relevant ideas to borrow from a number of designs.

For example, the plans for Site Seven show four different interpretations of a landscape full of outdoor recreation ideas. Whether you need a play space for kids or you're more interested in entertaining grown-ups, you should be able to find exactly what you want among the many choices these designers created.

Good design is the result of good planning. The landscapes you admire are the result of creative thought, compromise, and inspiration. Let these designs get you started.

Some landscapes emphasize permanence and formality, even while providing built-in play for grown-ups and children alike. This plan (left) includes a shady patio for entertaining adjacent to a pool and spa to be enjoyed by all; because hardscapes dominate, the look is easy to sustain.

Soft plantings and a homey brick walk invite neighbors and friends into this landscape (right) and welcome the owners at the end of the day. Informal beds of blooms brighten this friendly site with color while communicating an air of informality and ease.

Some landscapes establish a sense of place, such as this garden of cacti surrounding a Southwestern home. The low moisture needs are well-suited to the environment, and the wide variety of plantings makes a walk through the garden fascinating.

Good planning can create a low-maintenance landscape. This well-conceived plan includes ample built-in storage for garden tools, easy to maintain hardscapes, and ground cover and other plantings that minimize mowing and trimming.

Even small lots can be well-utilized for family interests. The side deck in this plan makes good use of limited space, providing play space for children and container gardening opportunities for adults. The well-planned deck is adjacent to the kitchen, uniting interior and exterior spaces, allowing parents to supervise younger children, and making a small herb garden convenient.

While some homeowners want low-maintenance plantings, others are avid gardeners and want landscapes designed for many growing opportunities. Beds for vegetables, perennials, and plantings designed to produce ample cut flowers for indoors can be incorporated into a plan for the garden hobbyist.

THE DESIGN PROCESS

Design is a problem-solving process that mixes what you like with what will work to make the most of any situation. It's important to remember that you don't have to implement an entire design at once; a plan will make your landscape appear unified when finished, so you can complete the work in phases as your budget allows. You may wish to consider consulting a professional for design assistance. A landscape architect or garden designer will discuss your needs, analyze your site, and suggest solutions you may not have thought of. You can pay an hourly fee for consultations or negotiate a flat rate for producing a set of drawings.

Step one in the design process is to create a wish and needs list— indicate the features you would like as wishes; those that are indispensable are needs. If it becomes necessary to simplify your plan to economize, some wishes can be eliminated or postponed.

Your landscape plan starts with a drawing of your property to scale; begin by sketching a base map that shows the outside dimensions of your house and the property lines; you can use the plot plan you received when you purchased your home for an easy reference.

GETTING STARTED

Begin by sketching a base map that shows the outside dimensions of your house and the perimeter lines of your property. Use a scale of ¼" or ⅛" = 1'-0" if your site is small; otherwise, use 1" =10'-0" scale. Your plan should fit on 24" × 36" paper. You can use the plot plan (also referred to as a survey or plat) that you received in your closing documents when you bought your home for a head start on these dimensions. Sketch on your base map to show features that are not going to change, such as walkways, walls, fences, patios, and plants you plan to keep. Note the location of doors, windows, service and utility features, including septic systems. Record the direction of prevailing winds, areas that are sunny or shady most of the year, low spots where drainage is poor, and views that need to be blocked or preserved.

Once you have a base plan, make several photocopies or use tracing paper overlays so you can make additions and subtractions without ruining your original. Now you can begin to play around with your design, considering the relationships between spaces you would like to have in your landscape. Use bubble diagrams like those shown on the opposite page for a quick way to explore various schemes. This stage is conceptual, so don't get bogged down trying to figure out any details. Scribble quick diagrams, moving bubbles to different areas of your site to discover the best possible combination of uses for your site. Review all the landscape plans in the following chapters to discover fresh ideas and solutions about how to use various parts of your landscape

Trace your best bubble diagram and use it as the basis for a concept diagram. This plan gives you a chance to apply ideas to your proposed bubbles. For example, an area labeled simply as *entertaining* on your bubble diagram may become the basis for a new patio on your concept diagram. Refine ideas and sketch them to scale to create the next step, a master plan. Once you have this, you can prepare detailed plans for planting and construction that show sizes, locations, and quantity of materials.

TIMING AND EXPERTISE

Now it's time to ask yourself a question: Do you plan to do most of the labor yourself? While landscaping your yard isn't the most difficult project you can undertake, it's more complex than planting a few shrubs. Evaluate the time and skills needed; you may decide to hire a landscape contractor to install the entire project or decide to use subcontractors to help with specific parts, doing other tasks yourself.

First, mark things you want to preserve, and then remove things such as trees and paving you didn't include in your new design. Complete any grading necessary and lay sleeves for conduit, future plumbing, and wiring before building hardscape projects. Stake new tree locations and mark bed-lines on the ground with lime or chalk dust to see your planting plan. Install underground sprinklers. Plant trees next, then shrubs and ground covers, followed by perennials, annuals, and lawn.

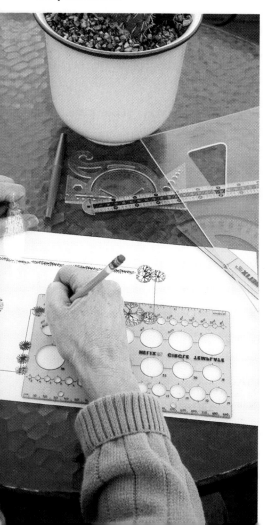

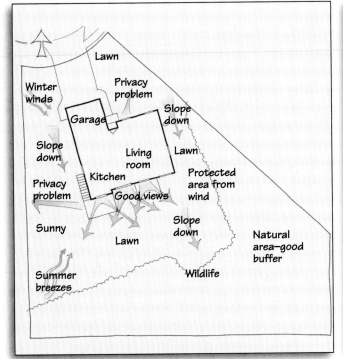

After you have drawn your base plan to scale, note features that will stay, views you wish to preserve or block, prevailing winds, and drainage on the property.

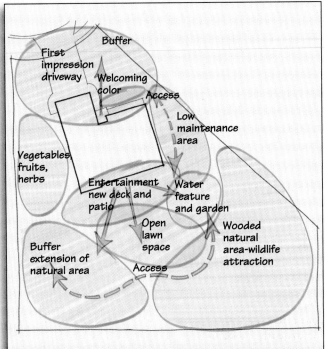

Next, evaluate the use of space by drawing bubble diagrams. These bubbles represent spaces within the landscape and how you plan to use them. Examine the relationship between areas on your site. After exploring a variety of bubble diagrams, settle on a favorite and then gradually shape the bubbles into actual solutions.

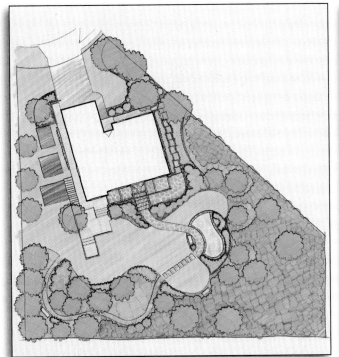

From the concept phase, develop a master plan, where you refine your ideas into actual objects, structures and plants drawn to scale. This provides a general blueprint to begin the implementation process.

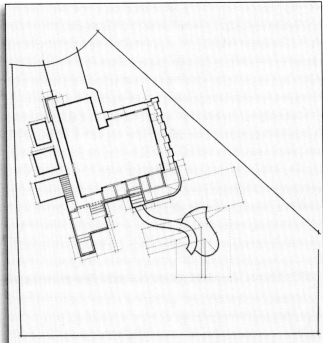

Finally, you develop a series of detailed plans for planting and construction that show sizes, locations, and quantity of plants and materials. Next, you will decide what you can do yourself and what you will need to hire experts to complete.

You'll want to consider many things before choosing your hardscape materials. Observe the very different moods set by these two gardens paths. The mortared brick path (left) is straight and formal. It is also expensive. The curving path of concrete aggregate (right) gives a more informal air to the garden. Walks of pea gravel or pavers set into sand are even more affordable, in part because they can easily be constructed by homeowners.

A trellised garden bench makes an attractive resting spot in the landscape; if you are on a limited budget, check with suppliers to see what woods are most available and affordable in your region.

MATERIALS AND ELEMENTS

A landscape plan combines hardscape elements (stone, concrete, wood) and living components (shrubs, trees, bedding plants) into a cohesive and visually appealing design that defines exterior space.

For walls, fences, and paving, material choices include gravel, stone, brick, concrete, and wood. Prices depend on availability of material in your area and the amount of labor required for installation. Brick and stone may be mortared to slabs or dry-laid on beds of sand or crushed rock. Decorative gravel can make attractive walks and seating areas that are easy to build. Concrete is a versatile material that can be dramatically altered in appearance by tinting wet mixes or staining finished surfaces. Stamping wet concrete can produce patterns resembling brick, cut stone, or cobblestone. Special treatments increase the square footage cost of concrete, but may prove less expensive than brick or stone.

Arbors, decks, and trellises are ideally constructed using redwood or cedar because of their natural resistance to rot. But other wood that costs considerably less can be used with good results. Pressure-treated pine is an economical alternative in many regions. The wood is impregnated with chemicals that protect it from decay in damp environments. Allow pressure-treated wood to weather before painting or staining. Use hot-dipped galvanized fasteners to prevent rust streaks.

Plant material represents a significant portion of a landscape budget. For this reason, you should build your design around species that prosper in your region. Don't be afraid to try unfamiliar plants, but minimize the roles of these experimental plants in your design to avoid disaster if they don't thrive.

Large shrubs are appealing because of their impressive size, but you can cut initial costs if you start with 1- or 3-gallon plants. Patience will prove that all plants eventually reach maturity, regardless of their original size. You may want to invest in a few large specimen plants for impact. Remember to space plants to allow for growth. When selecting plants, consider foliage color, texture and plant forms to give your landscape unity through repetition and accent through contrast.

Plant materials represent a significant portion of your landscape budget; select plantings with care to determine what thrives in your climate as well as what grows best in specific areas of your site.

LANDSCAPE PARAMETERS

Creating a successful landscape is an exercise in problem-solving. As the designer of your project, your goal is to fashion an outdoor environment that is comfortable and functional for everyone who uses it. Use landscaping material as windbreaks to deflect or channel harsh breezes away from the house or outdoor rooms. Sheltering trees and overhead structures transform hot spots into shady retreats. Buffers are useful for reducing noise and glare and can be achieved by planting layers of trees and shrubs; combining plants with solid walls creates a complete buffer. The sound of moving water can mask noises and create a pleasant ambience.

Both privacy and security are priorities for many families. Establishing degrees of privacy can create intimate areas as well as public spaces within your landscape. Strategically placed evergreen trees and shrubs can block views year-round to create privacy or hide utilitarian items. Deciduous trees or shrubs establish a sense of separation but still allow some visibility. Depending upon height, walls and fences can create cozy courtyards or welcoming entry gardens.

Good landscape design can give a small yard the illusion of spaciousness. Establishing a background and directing views inward to a detailed area makes the most of a small site. Placing coarse textures in the foreground and fine textures in the back can increase the perception of space. Concealing part of an area from view gives the impression that space continues indefinitely. On the other hand, an overwhelmingly large yard can appear more intimate if you establish zones of use. Walls aren't necessary to create garden rooms; let plantings, changes in elevation, paving patterns, and arbors define space.

Use design to convert problems to assets. For example, you can divert water from a wet area to create a spot suitable for a planting bed. Or, accentuate the site's characteristics by directing other drainage to this spot and then lining it with river stone. Plant water-loving plants that will thrive in the damp soil.

The right plant in the right place can reduce time spent pruning and pampering.

A good landscape will be well used. Your plan should include thought about the atmosphere you wish to create, as well as specific solutions to deflect harsh wind, provide shade, and create tranquility with privacy, attractive surroundings, and noise buffers.

Fences create privacy and security, but with a little thought, they can also contribute beauty to the landscape. Fast-growing vines, or planters full of blooms and cascading foliage can add color and texture to perimeter fencing for little expense and effort.

Design converts problems to assets. A troublesome rock outcropping can become the backdrop for a delightful naturalized garden with effective planning.

WORKING WITHIN YOUR MEANS

Good landscaping is not cheap. A commonly accepted rule is that you should invest 10 percent to 15 percent of your home's value in landscaping. That's from $11,000 to $16,500 for a home worth $110,000. This amount should cover more than plants. You may need additional parking, an outdoor entertaining area, fencing, walkways, and landscape lighting. Prioritize your needs for the inside and outside of your house. Spending money on your landscape may solve indoor design problems less expensively than making architectural changes. You can enhance entries, enlarge living spaces, improve interior privacy, reduce energy costs, increase natural light, redirect routes through rooms, and change the functions of rooms by improving interior and exterior relationships.

Producing plans will make it possible to determine how expensive your dreams are. Make a copy of your design and mark through items as you tally materials. List sizes and quantities of plants. Calculate square footage of hardscape items and list alternative materials. Reputable contractors and nurseries can help you determine related expenses. Always obtain at least three bids. Request unit prices to be sure you are comparing apples to apples. Make sure each contractor understands the scope of work to avoid

Stick to your budget when ordering plants from catalogs. It's easy to get carried away!

hidden costs later. Remember to include such items as mulch and fertilizer and easy-to-overlook expenses including demolition, hauling, and stump grinding when calculating totals. If you're planning to hire someone to do the work for you, ask if there are ways to reduce costs. Changing plant sizes can make quite a difference if you are purchasing large quantities. Substituting one plant for another can save money, too. Ask contractors if they have a slow season when their prices are reduced. Doing site work ahead of time may also save money. Ask what prep work you can do and how much you can save. Removing old plants, lawn, and concrete may be a worthwhile endeavor. Having a nursery deliver and place a large tree in a hole you've already dug may cost less than hiring a contractor to go get the tree and plant it for you. Buy small plants and give them a good start with soil amendments, fertilizer, and water and watch them flourish.

If prices are still beyond your reach, take another look at your design. Search for compromises that will preserve the integrity of your ideas. For instance, if you can't afford the brick walkway you designed, consider pouring a concrete walk and laying strips of brick between sections or along the sides as a decorative border. Slim down planting areas to keep the same bed shape but reduce the area that requires new plants.

You can also plan to do the work in phases. This allows you to spend money as your budget allows. Because you are filling in parts of an overall plan, your landscape won't have an added-on look even though it is installed over a period of time.

Scheduling a landscape project takes some planning. It's important to do things in the

PERMITS AND RESTRICTIONS

For some landscape projects, you may need a permit from the city before construction can begin. As a rule, cities have adapted their codes from the Uniform Building Code, which was written to enhance public safety and protect property owners from unsafe construction. Local codes take precedence, so it's important to check with planning and zoning boards. For example, a local code that has stricter requirements for pool enclosures is legally enforceable even if the Uniform Building Code has been satisfied. Projects that may require permits include curb cuts to install a driveway, electrical work such as upgrading a service panel or outdoor wiring, tree removal, walls over 30" high, decks, patios, and some plumbing work. Check with your local building department to determine if you need a permit for your proposed project. You or your contractor should also check with the city to determine if there are any zoning ordinances, easements, or setbacks that may affect your landscape design. Homeowners' associations may have to review your plan for compliance with rules regarding fences, walls, paint or stain colors, setbacks, planting design, irrigation systems, and drainage.

Grading shapes the soil to accommodate the new design; it may require professional help.

need to do some fine grading by hand with a steel rake. While they are still in their containers, set trees and shrubs in proposed beds to double-check quantities and bed sizes. Make adjustments as needed. Plant trees first so you'll have room to maneuver. Set shrubs in place and plant along the bed-line first to establish the shape, working your way back through the bed. If you are aligning some of the plants with a structure behind the bed, such as a wall or trellis, set those plants when you start along the bed-line and meet in the middle. Do the same for ground covers and perennials. Always mulch and water new plants as they are planted to prevent them from drying out. Lawns and annuals are last.

proper order to avoid damaging new installations. If you are managing several contractors, prepare a timeline to direct the work to avoid costly repairs and replacements along the way. Consider offering bonuses for timeliness, or include in your contract the ability to reduce payment as penalty for avoidable schedule delays.

Start by clearly identifying existing items you want to preserve and things you want to remove from your property. Establish a construction entrance to prevent heavy equipment from cracking paving, damaging planting beds and lawn, or parking beneath trees. Pick a holding area for plants that is near a water source and won't expose plants to full sun or heavy shade. Make certain delivery drivers know how to access your property and where to leave materials.

Grading comes next. Earth work may be necessary to shape the soil to accommodate new features of your design. Always make sure you have positive drainage so water will flow away from the foundation of your house and other structures. Paving and soil should slope enough to shed water instead of collecting it. A 2 percent slope will move stormwater off patios, driveways, and walks, without a noticeable pitch. After grading, lay conduit to serve as sleeves for wiring and small pipes that may need to pass through areas of construction. This will save you from having to bore under paving and structures later.

Hardscape items such as decks, arbors, walkways, driveways, and patios are built when grading is completed. If large trees will be planted inside a hardscape area, set trees first so paving will not be damaged by equipment needed to move the tree.

Install underground systems next. Lighting and irrigation should be in place before planting begins so trenching won't damage progress. Always flag utilities prior to digging.

Lay a garden hose on the ground or use lime to represent your new bed-lines. You may

HOW TO WORK WITH A PRO

If you decide you want professional input, there are several avenues worth exploring. You can purchase plans from a designer who has no vested interest in profit from construction; you may have a design prepared from a nursery, which includes the plans as part of the sale of plants; or you can work with a design-build firm that folds the cost of design into the construction of the project.

Titles can be confusing. A *landscape architect* is a degreed professional who has passed national and state licensing tests. This title may not be used by anyone who has not met these requirements. If in doubt, ask to see a registration number. Landscape architects study design, construction, plants, grading, irrigation, and spatial relationships. Some landscape architects specialize in residential design while others do only commercial projects. Ask to see completed projects before commissioning design work. Establish in your contract whether the landscape architect will be on hand during construction. You may purchase plans only or you can pay for site observation. That's when a landscape architect will inspect materials and installations and approve payment requests and change orders submitted by contractors. Some landscape architects also own design-build enterprises and will act as contractor on the project.

Landscape designers and *garden designers* do not usually have to meet any formal requirements to practice their skills. Many specialize in planting design for private homes. Some will procure plants or provide labor as well.

Landscape contractors work from plans that others prepare. They can bid on projects to give you an installation estimate. Some landscape contractors will only do planting; others will oversee development of the entire project, from demolition and grading to irrigation, hardscape construction, and planting; some will even provide ongoing maintenance. Design-build contractors retain landscape architects or designers on staff to prepare plans. There may not be a charge for these designs, but you are expected to use the same firm for installation.

Always clearly define the scope of work in any contract you sign, whether for design work or for materials and labor. Specify that any deviations from the plans can only proceed with a change order approved and signed by you. Retain at least 10 percent of payment pending a final project inspection.

HOW TO USE THIS BOOK

To help you develop a landscape that meets your personal needs, 28 of America's leading landscape architects and designers have come together to offer you a wealth of design ideas.

In each of the following seven chapters, a typical landscape site is described. For each site, four designers from different regions create four unique plans for solving the problems of the site and maximizing its assets.

While the basic site remains the same for each of the four designs in a chapter, the objectives, architectural style, and regional context shift considerably. The result is a wide range of styles, approaches and regional solutions for the same set of problems—with a wealth of ideas to fit your needs, whatever your property and wherever you live.

While you will find ideas in every plan in this book that can be adapted to your property, the lists on this page make it easy for you to turn to plans that directly relate to your landscape objectives and your region, as well as certain features and planting solutions.

LANDSCAPE OBJECTIVES

Each design in this book has been created to fulfill 28 different pairs of the eight major categories of landscape objectives described and illustrated below. Of course, any successful landscape will fulfill all eight objectives at once. But identifying their relative importance and concentrating on the ones most important to you is an excellent way to direct your design. For plans that meet the particular objectives you hope to achieve, consult the following pages:

Fun: For an outdoor world replete with tree houses, play areas, putting greens, pools, and sport courts, see these pages: 23, 33, 37, 53, 61, 73, 83.

Relaxation: For a retreat from a hectic world, a quiet, tranquil place that fosters meditation and solitude, see these pages: 19, 29, 39, 47, 59, 69, 79.

Nature: Why trek to the country when you can have it in the backyard? For natural designs with native plants, see pages: 17, 31, 41, 49, 61, 71, 79.

Welcome: For the landscape that beckons visitors with friendly entrances and neighborly connections, see pages: 21, 29, 43, 49, 57, 73, 81.

Beauty: For the pictorial landscape that is a feast for the senses, with impressive views of lush, elegant plantings and features, see pages: 17, 27, 37, 47, 57, 67, 77.

Convenience: For landscape plans filled with conveniences for easy living such as storage space, good indoor-outdoor access, and easy maintenance, see pages: 19, 31, 43, 51, 63, 67, 83.

Gardening: For landscapes for the hands-on gardener, filled with flowers, vegetable plots and fruit orchards or herb, cut-flower, and Alpine gardens, see pages: 21, 33, 39, 53, 63, 71, 77.

Entertaining: For sociable landscapes built to entertain, with outdoor kitchen, dining facilities, seating, and pavilions, often with night-lighting and a fireplace, see pages: 23, 27, 41, 51, 59, 69, 81.

REGIONS

Where you live governs what plants you can grow, as well as which materials will prove durable. But successful landscapes also blend with their surroundings to achieve a good fit with regional context, aesthetics and style. This can mean using plants native to your area, as well as building materials (such as stone) that are locally available. It can also lead you to choose a style and approach appropriate to your region.

REGIONAL PLANS:

Northwest: 31, 67, 81
West: 27, 41, 45, 51, 53, 61
Southwest: 23, 57, 59, 79
Southeast: 19, 43, 47, 69, 71, 77
Midwest: 17, 33, 37, 49, 73
Northeast: 21, 29, 35, 39, 63, 83

SPECIAL PLANTING NEEDS

These plans will help you with decisions about seasonal color, drought tolerance, a need for barriers or kitchen gardens.

Seasonal color: 17, 19, 21, 29, 31, 33, 37, 39, 41, 43, 49, 51, 53, 59, 61, 63, 67, 69, 71, 73, 77, 79, 81, 83
Drought tolerance: 23, 49, 51, 53, 57, 61, 79

Good barriers: 19, 33, 37, 41, 43, 47, 51, 53, 59, 63, 67, 71
Kitchen gardens: 17, 23, 31, 33, 39, 41, 53, 63, 67, 69, 73, 77, 79, 81, 83

FEATURES

There is a wealth of imaginative features contained in the 28 landscape designs in this book. To help you locate specific structural features, consult the plans on the pages listed below.

Fencing, Gates: 17, 19, 21, 27, 31, 59, 63, 67, 71, 73, 77, 81, 83

Patios, Decks: 17, 19, 23, 27, 29, 31, 33, 37, 41, 43, 47, 49, 51, 53, 57, 59, 61, 67, 69, 71, 73, 81, 83

Water Features: 17, 27, 29, 37, 41, 43, 47, 49, 53, 57, 59, 61, 67, 71, 73

Planters, Raised Beds: 19, 23, 49, 51, 53, 59, 61, 67, 69, 71, 79, 81, 83

Storage: 33, 51, 59, 61, 63, 71, 73

Trellises, Arbors, Pergolas: 17, 19, 23, 33, 37, 41, 43, 47, 49, 51, 53, 57, 59, 61, 63, 71, 73, 77

Barbecues, Firepits, Fireplaces: 23, 41, 61

Play Areas: 23, 29, 33, 41, 53, 73

Pools, Spas: 19, 21, 33, 61, 69

Wheelchair Access: 71

N

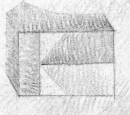

Overhead view shows the quarter-acre site with a 1,500 sq. ft. single-story house and detached garage. The outdated kidney-shaped pool is visible in the rear patio. Because the lot is on an intersection, and the set-back house is close to others, privacy and security are important issues.

SITE ONE: OLDER SUBURBAN HOME ON CORNER LOT

This landscape setting is typical of millions of homes across the country—an older, suburban corner lot with a modest, single-story house set back from the intersecting streets. The property is level, and about ¼-acre in size. Sidewalks border both streets, and the corner serves as a school bus stop. Neighboring houses are close by, and there is a narrow, unused stretch of property along the kitchen and dining room side of the house.

The first impression of the house is greatly influenced by the landscaping, giving this home a dated look. From the abundance of overgrown and neglected shrubs along the foundation and property lines to the kidney-shaped swimming pool in the backyard, everything seems out of style, almost to the point of neglect.

A new approach to landscaping is essential to increase curb appeal. Privacy and security need to be improved, and pedestrians must be discouraged from cutting across the yard. Traffic noise and headlight glare are problems that affect the house and the grounds. The large front yard is an impersonal and exposed area. The lawn is shapeless and indistinct from neighboring properties. The lack of color and texture leaves the yard lacking in personality and easy to pass by. There is nothing to call attention to the front door. Throughout the property, exterior spaces have no function or destination, making the landscape nothing more than an area that requires mowing.

In this landscape solution, privacy plantings and low-maintenance beds offer separation from the street. A trellis (top) beckons visitors to the new patio off the kitchen/dining rooms.

Barrier & Screening
Japanese barberry
(Berberis thunbergii)
Juniper
(Juniperus spp.)
Lilac
(Syringa vulgaris)
European cranberry
(Viburnum opulus)

Grasses & Ground Covers
Little bluestem
(Andropogon scoparius)
Purple-leaf wintercreeper
(Euonymus fortunei 'Coloratus')
Blue fescue
(Festuca ovina 'Glauca')
Singleseed juniper
(Juniperus squamata 'Blue Carpet')
Prairie dropseed
(Sporobolus heterolepis)
Sod Grower II Kentucky Blue mix for Northern Iowa
Super Turf 2 Fescue Blue mix for Southern Iowa

Patio trellis

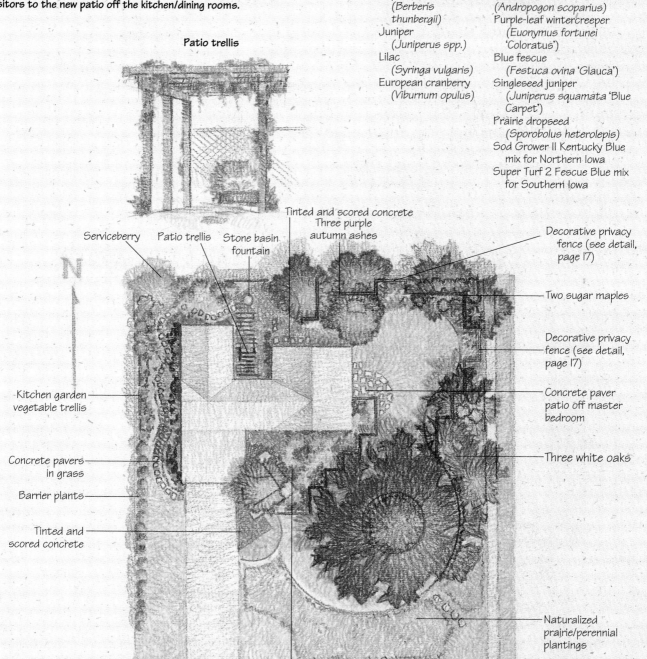

Serviceberry   Patio trellis   Stone basin fountain

Tinted and scored concrete
Three purple autumn ashes

Decorative privacy fence (see detail, page 17)

Two sugar maples

Decorative privacy fence (see detail, page 17)

Concrete paver patio off master bedroom

Three white oaks

Kitchen garden vegetable trellis

Concrete pavers in grass

Barrier plants

Tinted and scored concrete

Naturalized prairie/perennial plantings

Entry, garden with low maintenance perennials, ground cover, and specimen trees

Shrubs
Serviceberry
(Amelanchier spp.)
Japanese barberry
(Berberis thunbergii)
Red-osier dogwood
(Cornus stolonifera)
Forsythia
(Forsythia spp.)
Spirea
(Spiraea spp.)
Lilac
(Syringa spp.)

Trees
Japanese maple
(Acer palmatum)
Sugar maple
(Acer saccharum)
Redbud
(Cercis canadensis)
White Ash
(Fraxinus americana 'Autumn Purple')
White oak
(Quercus alba)

Beds & Borders
Bugleweed
(Ajuga spp.)
Horsetail milkweed,
(Asclepias verticillata)
Heath aster
(Aster ericoides)
Smooth aster
(A. laevis)
Shasta daisy
(Leucanthemum × superbum)

Coreopsis
(Coreopsis spp.)
Pink coneflower
(Echinacea pallida)
Daylily
(Hemerocallis spp.)
Hosta
(Hosta spp.)
Dyersweed goldenrod
(Solidago nemoralis)
Lamb's ears
(Stachys byzantina)

DES MOINES, IOWA
BEAUTY AND NATURE
by John Crose, Landscape Architect, RDG Crose Gardner Shukert, Des Moines, Iowa

John Crose designed this informal style landscape solution for first-time homeowners: a couple in their thirties with three elementary school-age children. It's an attractive landscape that requires little time and expertise to maintain for a busy family. The budget of $5,000 excludes pool renovation.

The large shade tree in front remains in the new design. Years of neglect made it more practical to remove overgrown shrubs than to salvage them. Filling the old pool eliminated a maintenance problem and created more lawn play space for the children.

A new walkway of tinted and scored concrete with 6-inch limestone edging leads invitingly to the entry through beds of carefree perennials, ground cover, and shrubs. A redbud and Japanese maple add accents. In addition to seasonal color, these deciduous trees shed leaves in autumn, which permits winter sunlight to enter the house.

Drifts of drought-tolerant perennials and seed-sown wildflowers create streetside interest. Screening shrubs and trees enhance privacy and help buffer traffic noise and glare.

The west-facing side yard, once wasted space, is the ideal spot for a kitchen garden.

Three 9-foot sections of trellis, built using 2 × 6 posts and beams, 1 × 2 bracing, and stainless steel cable in eye hooks, are perfect for climbers such as cucumbers. Concrete pavers lead to a new patio, trellis, and stone basin water feature, creating a new outdoor destination.

A decorative stepped fence provides an additional level of privacy as well as visual interest along the southeastern corner.

The front yard viewed from a corner of the property illustrates how naturalized prairie and perennial planting beds were designed to create a focal point under the branches of the regal white oak.

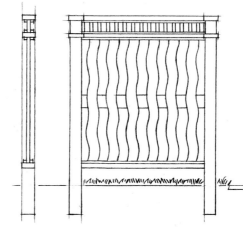

A section of the fencing designed for the eastern boundary of the site

This design employs handsome hedging and specimen trees for privacy and security. The pergola will be covered with roses (top detail).

Grasses & Ground Covers
Variegated English ivy
  (Hedera helix 'Elegance')
Yellow archangel
  (Lamium galeobdolon
  'Herman's Pride')
Periwinkle
  (Vinca minor)

Barrier & Screening
Common boxwood
  (Buxus
  sempervirens)
Hyacinth bean,
  (Dolichos lablab)
Burning bush
  (Euonymus alata)
Holly
  (Ilex spp.)
Everblooming
  honeysuckle
  (Lonicera heckrottii)
Rose, shrub and
  climbing
  (Rosa spp.)

Pergola with Pink Climbing Roses

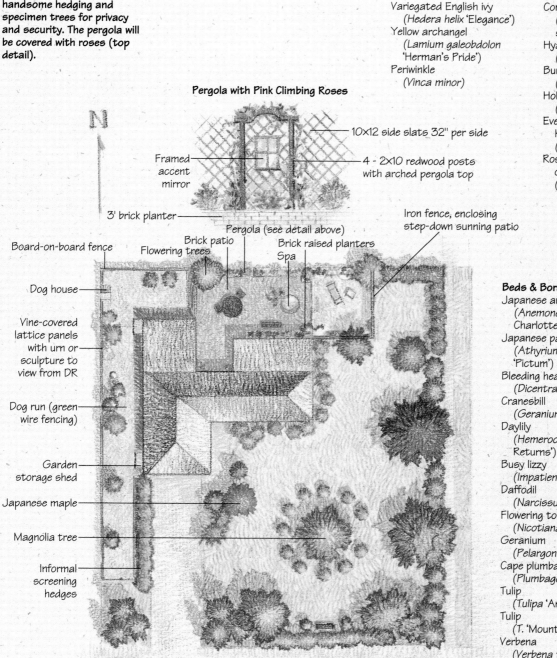

Framed accent mirror

10x12 side slats 32" per side

4 - 2x10 redwood posts with arched pergola top

3' brick planter

Pergola (see detail above)

Iron fence, enclosing step-down sunning patio

Board-on-board fence

Flowering trees

Brick patio

Brick raised planters

Spa

Dog house

Vine-covered lattice panels with urn or sculpture to view from DR

Dog run (green wire fencing)

Garden storage shed

Japanese maple

Magnolia tree

Informal screening hedges

Beds & Borders
Japanese anemone
  (Anemone × hybrida 'Queen
  Charlotte')
Japanese painted fern
  (Athyrium nipponicum
  'Pictum')
Bleeding heart
  (Dicentra eximia 'Snowdrift')
Cranesbill
  (Geranium 'Claridge Druce')
Daylily
  (Hemerocallis 'Happy
  Returns')
Busy lizzy
  (Impatiens spp.)
Daffodil
  (Narcissus 'Actaea')
Flowering tobacco
  (Nicotiana spp.)
Geranium
  (Pelargonium spp.)
Cape plumbago
  (Plumbago auriculata)
Tulip
  (Tulipa 'Angelique')
Tulip
  (T. 'Mount Tacoma')
Verbena
  (Verbena tenuisecta 'Edith')

Trees

Threadleaf Japanese maple
  (Acer palmatum dissectum)
Chinese fringe tree
  (Chionanthus retusus)
Dogwood
  (Cornus spp.)
Foster's holly
  (Ilex attenuata 'Fosterii')
Crape myrtle
  (Lagerstroemia 'Natchez')

Dwarf southern magnolia
  (Magnolia grandiflora 'Little
  Gem')
Japanese flowering crab apple
  (Malus floribunda)
Flowering plum
  (Prunus cerasifera
  'Thundercloud')
Chaste tree
  (Vitex agnus-castus 'Alba')

Beautyberry
  (Callicarpa bodinieri 'Alba')
Autumn-blooming camellia
  (Camellia sasanqua 'Snow
  Flurry')
Summersweet
  (Clethra alnifloia 'Rosea')
Cranberry cotoneaster
  (Cotoneaster apiculatus)
Winter daphne
  (Daphne odora)

Shrubs

Winged euonymus
  (Euonymus alata)
Mountain laurel hybrids
  (Kalmia latifolia)
Mugo pine
  (Pinus mugo mugo)
Azalea
  (Rhododendron spp.)
Viburnum
  (Viburnum x burkwoodii)

ALEXANDRIA, VIRGINIA
RELAXATION AND CONVENIENCE
by Ann E. Schmidtlein, Landscape Designer, Alexandria, Virginia

Ann E. Schmidtlein's design for this site suits a childless young couple who owns a dog and dislikes yard work. "Peaceful living is an overriding objective for these homeowners," Ann observes.

Because the initial budget was limited to $5,000, Ann concentrated on setting up a schedule of improvements that spans two or three years. For the first phase, most of the overgrown shrubs and trees are removed and a new palette of low-maintenance plantings added—shrubs that don't require formal shearing and perennials that won't need dividing for years. The lawn area will be gradually eliminated and replaced by white gravel. A 6-foot board-on-board fence and shielding trees along the back property line add privacy right away. Trees and shrubs planted along the perimeter of both streets provide valuable screening. A rose-covered pergola and lush, sheltering plantings enclose an outdoor entertaining area and future spa.

Ann designed the garden for a traditional-style white brick house commonly found in her region, developing an English garden theme—many fragrant species with soft colors and loose, natural forms. Her concept is of a charming, somewhat romantic garden full of white and pastel colors united by a repetition of materials.

Future phases begin by replacing the pool with a spa. The filled-in pool cavity will be paved with brick to create an outdoor dining area. Next, brick will be laid over pavement, providing two steps down to an adjacent gravel sitting area. A single lantern beside the step will be added for safety. A storage shed is third on the list of future features. Finally, an in-ground automated sprinkler system for the front and east plantings will make watering a chore of the past while keeping plants lush.

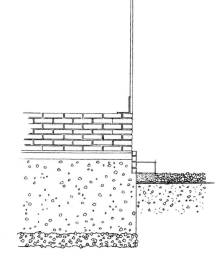

A new brick patio includes brick planters. Two steps lead from the patio to the gravel sitting area.

Dramatic island beds add interest in this simply elegant landscape solution. New stone paving creates a welcoming entry and is softened by a sweeping area of greenscape.

Barrier & Screening

Nootka false cypress
  (*Chamaecyparis nootkatensis* 'Pendula')
Leyland cypress
  (× *Cupressocyparis leylandii*)
Climbing hydrangea,
  (*Hydrangea anomala petiolaris*)
Holly
  (*Ilex spp.*)
Serbian spruce
  (*Picea omorika*)

Blue limber pine
  (*Pinus flexilis glauca*)
Bosnian pine
  (*P. heldreichii leucodermis*)
American arborvitae
  (*Thuja occidentalis* 'Pyramidalis' or 'Wintergreen')
Western red cedar
  (*Thuya plicata*)

Upgraded pool coping

New privacy fence
(see detail page 21)

Teen retreat (see
illustration page 21)

Pines

Kitchen/dining patio

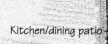

N

Additional concrete
turf block parking

Barrier/screening plants

Courtesy bus
stop bench

Birdbath or small
water feature

Perennial bed

Bluestone entry walk

Trees

Swiss stone pine
  (*Pinus cembra*)
Scotch pine
  (*P. sylvestris* 'Fastigiata')

Bench placed on corner
with backdrop of
flowering shrubs
and perennials makes a
nice place to wait for
the school bus.

Shrubs

Japanese barberry
  (*Berberis thunbergii* 'Rose Glow')
Butterfly bush
  (*Buddleja davidii*)
Dwarf sawara false cypress
  (*Chamaecyparis pisifera* 'Filifera Nana')
Forsythia
  (*Forsythia* × *intermedia* 'Spectabilis')
Vernal witch hazel
  (*Hamamelis vernalis*)

St. John's wort
  (*Hypericum* 'Hidcote')
Holly
  (*Ilex* 'Nellie R. Stevens')
Dwarf mountain laurel
  (*Kalmia latifolia* 'Minuet')
Japanese kerria
  (*Kerria japonica*)
Coast leucothoe
  (*Leucothoe axillaris*)

Lily-of-the-valley bush
  (*Pieris japonica* 'Dorothy Wyckoff')
Exbury azalea hybrids
  (*Rhododendron spp.*)
Lilac
  (*Syringa vulgaris*)
Doublefile viburnum
  (*Viburnum plicatum tomentosum*)

SKILLMAN, NEW JERSEY
WELCOME AND GARDENING
by Michael Mitchell, Mitchell & Company, Skillman, New Jersey

The large yard is likely to attract a family with teenagers to this home. A budget of $6,000 to be spent over three years was established for giving the outdoor spaces a new, inviting look. "Our goal was to create a useful and visually interesting landscape," Michael Mitchell recalls.

In the front, a freeform island bed of annuals, perennials, conifers, and shrubs with different seasons of interest sets the theme for the new design. To give the entry more prominence, a generously curved terrace of bluestone replaces the concrete slab. This decorative paving updates the front door area and adds a welcoming air. Conifers and shrubs replace old, overgrown material along the home's foundation. Turf blocks provide additional parking.

The plan makes the backyard an area of activity. An outdoor dining area off the kitchen was designed with casual meals in mind. Although the pool was old and its coping in need of repair, it could be considered an asset by a family with older children. More attractive clay pavers replace the damaged concrete coping, a project that can be undertaken by the homeowner to keep the project on budget while retaining the pool. Resurfacing the pool is to be accomplished by a local pool contractor.

A new poolside sitting area makes the spot more inviting and is perfect for the teen social scene.

A mixture of conifers, such as pine, cedar, cypress, and arborvitae, provide year-round privacy. The evergreen plantings transform the large, impersonal lot into a series of outdoor rooms for family retreats. The sense of seclusion is enhanced by the installation of Princeton privacy fences at key locations in the yard.

Holly, barberry, viburnum, and andromeda add color and texture to the once-plain landscape.

A backyard nook is tucked among greenery for privacy and comfort (above). The Princeton privacy fence is constructed of red cedar (below).

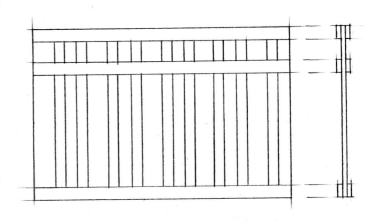

Extensive privacy buffers block traffic noise and views. A child's sheltered play area with covered sandbox and benches features hidden storage (top).

Beds & Borders

Sago palm
  (Cycas revoluta)
Holly fern
  (Cyrtomium falcatum)
Daylily
  (Hemerocallis spp.)
Iris
  (Iris spp.)
Dwarf crape myrtle
  (Lagerstroemia indica
  Petite Pinkie™ or Petite
  Snow™)

Big blue lily turf
  (Liriope muscari)
Banana
  (Musa velutina or Musa
  acuminata 'Dwarf
  Cavendish')
Cape plumbago
  (Plumbago auriculata)
Japanese yew
  (Taxus cuspidata)
Windmill palm
  (Trachycarpus fortunei
  'Nanus' and 'Capitata')

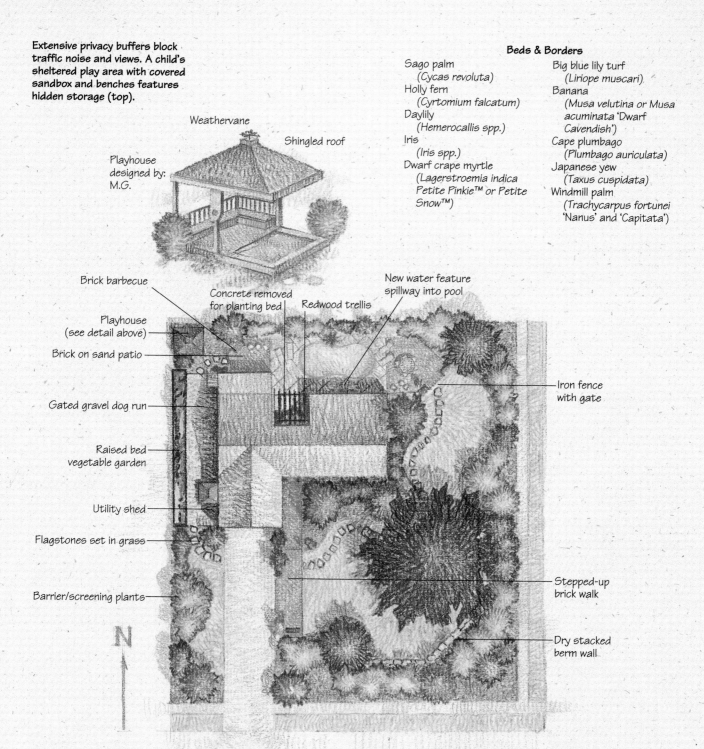

Weathervane

Shingled roof

Playhouse designed by: M.G.

Brick barbecue

Concrete removed for planting bed

Redwood trellis

New water feature spillway into pool

Playhouse (see detail above)

Brick on sand patio

Iron fence with gate

Gated gravel dog run

Raised bed vegetable garden

Utility shed

Flagstones set in grass

Barrier/screening plants

Stepped-up brick walk

Dry stacked berm wall

N

Trees
Mexican redbud
  (Cercis canadensis mexicana)
Western redbud)
  (C. occidentalis)
Bronze loquat
  (Eriobotrya deflexa)
Crape myrtle
  (Lagerstroemia indica)
California wax myrtle
  (Myrica californica)
Carolina cherry laurel
  (Prunus caroliniana)

Shrubs
Dwarf yaupon holly
  (Ilex vomitoria 'Nana' or
  'Stokes' Dwarf')
Mountain laurel
  (Kalmia latifolia)
Texas sage, or silverleaf
  (Leucophyllum frutescens)
Heavenly bamboo
  (Nandina domestica)
Dwarf Japanese mock orange
  (Pittosporum tobira
  'Wheeler's Dwarf')
Indian hawthorn
  (Rhaphiolepis indica)

Barrier & Screening
Surinam cherry
  (Eugenia uniflora)
Texas privet
  (Ligustrum japonicum
  'Texanum')
Oleander
  (Nerium oleander)
Fraser photinia
  (Photinia × fraseri)
Mock orange
  (Pittosporum tobira)
Xylosma
  (Xylosma congestum)

Grasses & Ground Covers
Buffalograss
  (Buchloe dactyloides)
Bermudagrass
  (Cynodon dactylon)
Lantana
  (Lantana montevidensis)
Mondo grass
  (Ophiopogon japonicus)
St. Augustinegrass
  (Stenotaphrum secundatum)
Asiatic jasmine
  (Trachelospermum asiaticum)

SAN ANTONIO, TEXAS
ENTERTAINING AND FUN
by David Elwell, Landscape Designer, Morris & White, Inc., San Antonio, Texas

David Elwell designed this plan for first-time homeowners in their mid-twenties with two toddlers and a live-in grandmother. The first year's landscape budget is limited to $5,000.

Safety and security from the street are high priorities in this plan. Small children in the family and a busy street on two sides of the property made fencing necessary in order for the yard to become usable. Outdoor storage for garden equipment and toys was essential, too. An outdoor destination where the family can cook and dine, and that could double as an entertainment area for friends and business associates, is incorporated into the plan.

To create visual interest, David uses curved beds and walkways which contrast with the rectilinear lines of existing hardscape. This theme is apparent throughout the landscape, beginning with the sweeping, 18-inch-high, dry-stacked stone retaining wall in the front yard. A curving flagstone path leads from a landing pad off the driveway to a new brick-on-sand patio outside the master bedroom.

The previously unused side yard along the west side of the house has been transformed into a multipurpose space. The location is just right for a storage area and a gravel dog run. There's even room for a vegetable and herb garden in a raised bed constructed of railroad ties. The proximity to the kitchen makes this small garden easy to tend and harvest.

Repetition of materials helps tie separate spaces together. Brick-on-sand construction forms a second patio in the northwest corner of the property. Here, the cookout center and dining space are adjacent to the kitchen for convenience. A trellised sitting area outside the kitchen and living room makes entertaining easy and comfortable.

Removing some of the pool decking created room for lush plantings that soften the hardscape. The plantings also add an air of intimacy to the backyard.

Future planting plans will claim the wasted front yard space for the family. Curving beds transition inward from the long, straight public sidewalks. Layers of plant materials add privacy and interest. The house will be glimpsed through a lush landscape, instead of seen all at once across a dull expanse of grass. This theme dramatically improves curb appeal. The curving bedlines also sculpt the lawn, forming a series of flowing spaces. The large shade tree, once alone in the big yard, becomes the largest component of a harmonious landscape.

The heavy privacy plantings incorporate welcoming walks and resting spots, (above). Dry stacked stone creates an attractive retaining wall (left).

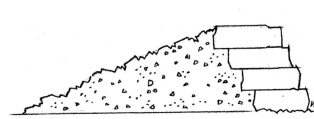

A bird's-eye perspective shows that privacy is paramount in this landscape. Blocking views from nearby neighbors and carving out secluded spaces in the rear garden are important design objectives.

N ←

SITE TWO: OLDER HOME, MIDTOWN LOT

This 1½ story, three-bedroom home of about 1,500 square feet was built in the 1920s or '30s. When new, the house was located on the outer suburban edge of the city, where land was plentiful and relatively inexpensive. The location is now considered midtown, the setting is urban, and by today's standard, the lot is small.

The narrow lot is rectangular, defined by a chain-link fence across the rear boundary. A long drive on the south side of the property leads from the street to a detached garage in the rear, a typical feature of houses this age.

Neighboring houses are close on every side; five neighbors' residences are visible from the back porch. Just two blocks away, miscellaneous shops and a few neighborhood-style restaurants flourish.

Problems that need solving are issues of privacy, security, and rehabilitating overgrown plantings—such as the tangle of neglected junipers overtaking the foundation.

The landscape needs a fresher look that will complement the old-house charm. Because the rear yard backs up to several neighbors, gaining privacy in that area is a primary concern. The side yard also needs screening to reclaim it for personal use from public view of passersby on the sidewalk.

Inadequate parking is another problem that needs to be addressed, without overwhelming the small front yard or the modest available landscaping budget.

With a welcoming new entrance and an intimate, inviting rear yard, this design makes good use of a limited budget. The lower detail shows a welcoming front entrance gate.

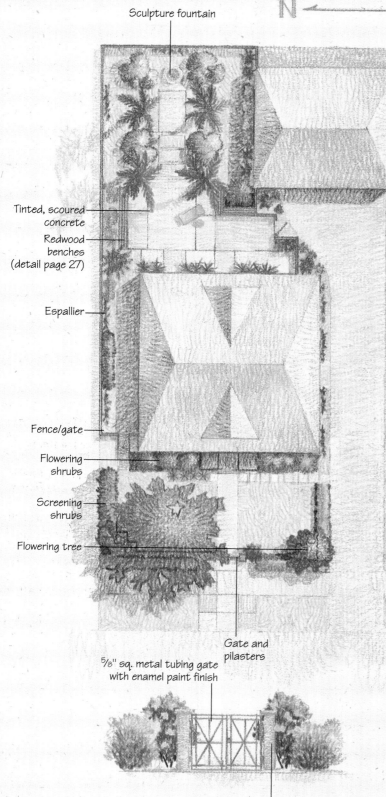

Sculpture fountain

N

Tinted, scoured concrete

Redwood benches (detail page 27)

Espallier

Fence/gate

Flowering shrubs

Screening shrubs

Flowering tree

Gate and pilasters

⁵⁄₈" sq. metal tubing gate with enamel paint finish

4' pilasters, stuccoed and color-coated to match house. Cap is 1' × 1' × 3" concrete

Trees

Hybrid strawberry tree (Arbutus 'Marina')

Bronze loquat (Eriobotrya deflexa)

Australian willow (Geijera parvifolia)

Dwarf southern magnolia (Magnolia grandiflora 'Little Gem'

Pygmy date palm (Phoenix roebelenii)

Purple-leaf plum (Prunus cerasifera 'Atropurpurea')

Ornamental pear (Pyrus calleryana)

Tupidanthus (Schefflera pueckleri)

Shrubs

Chinese hibiscus (Hibiscus rosa-sinensis)

Arabian jasmine (Jasminum sambac)

Dwarf heavenly bamboo (Nandina domestica 'Nana Purpurea')

Dwarf carnation-flowered pomegranate (Punica granatum 'Chico')

Dwarf yeddo hawthorn (Rhaphiolepis umbellata 'Minor')

Barrier & Screening

Japanese boxwood, (Buxus microphylla japonica)

Common camellia, (Camellia japonica)

Surinam cherry, (Eugenia uniflora)

Dwarf pittosporum (Pittosporum tobira 'Wheeler's Dwarf')

English cherry laurel, (Prunus laurocerasus)

Dwarf cherry laurel, (P. l. 'Nana')

Scarlet firethorn, (Pyracantha coccinea)

Madagascar jasmine, (Stephanotis floribunda)

Beds & Borders

Lady's mantle (Alchemilla mollis)

Daylily (Hemerocallis 'Stella d'Oro')

Coral bells (Heuchera 'Palace Purple')

Plantain lily (Hosta hybrid 'Sum and Substance')

Plantain lily (H. sieboldiana 'Elegans')

Siberian iris (Iris sibirica)

Peony (Paeonia)

Russian sage, (Perovskia atriplicifolia 'Superba')

Grasses & Ground Covers

Bearberry or kinnikinnick (Arctostaphylos uva-ursi 'Massachusetts')

Sweet woodruff (Galium odoratum)

Creeping Jenny (Lysimachia nummularia)

Creeping thyme (Thymus praecox arcticus)

Periwinkle (Vinca major)

LA JOLLA, CALIFORNIA
BEAUTY AND ENTERTAINING
by Jeff Stone, Landscape Architect, Jeff Stone Associates, La Jolla, California

Jeff Stone designed this plan for a professional and his artist wife in their early thirties. Yard size would be an asset, with possibilities for turning the property into an ideal home and studio where they could host frequent gatherings of friends and clients. The $7,500 landscape budget must address privacy issues and create abundant outdoor amenities. "I sought to create a crisp, sophisticated design for the front entry and patios, taking into account the small spaces and modest budget available," Jeff explains.

He began at the street, pouring a new landing of scored, tinted concrete which he repeated at the entry. Along the front public walk, Jeff added a low hedge to define the property boundary. A dwarf magnolia serves as a corner accent. Panels of lawn on each side of the entry walk contrast with the hot colors of flowering shrubs and perennials along the foundation. Beds of flowering and foliage plants soften the driveway to the south. Espaliers trained against the existing fence provide vertical interest and a pleasant view from bedroom windows. A lawn area provides a transition into the back garden.

New patios provide plenty of room for entertaining. Built-in benches for additional seating divide the patios into irregular shapes. Tinting and saw-cutting minimizes the impact of the expansive paving on the landscape. Jeff also suggested new doors at the back of the house for easy indoor-outdoor flow.

Surrounded by espaliered shrubs and bronze loquats, sculpture and a fountain become alluring focal points for the backyard.

A sequestered patio is surrounded with dense evergreen vegetation. Below is a detail drawing of redwood benches.

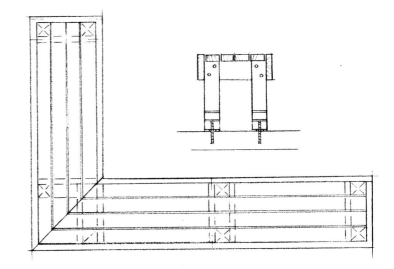

Attention to detail shows in this creative landscape solution, from the inviting stone entry courtyard (close-up, page 29) to the lovely rear garden with play area, where a children's playhouse provides lighthearted fun.

Shrubs

Burning bush
(Euonymus alata)
Panicle hydrangea
Hydrangea paniculata 'Tardiva'
Common winterberry
(Ilex verticillata)
Hybrid azalea
(Rhododendron 'Northern Lights')
Hardy evergreen rhododendron
(R. 'PJM Compact')

Polyantha rose
(Rosa 'The Fairy')
American elderberry
(Sambucus canadensis)
False spirea
(Sorbaria sorbifolia)
Garland spirea
(Spiraea × arguta)
Spiraea japonica 'Anthony Waterer'
Common lilac
(Syringa vulgaris)

Trees

Saucer magnolia
(Magnolia × soulangiana)
Serbian spruce
(Picea omorika)
Columnar English oak
(Quercus robur 'Fastigiata')

Beds & Borders

Lady's mantle
(Alchemilla mollis)
Daylily
(Hemerocallis 'Stella d'Oro')
Coral bell
(Heuchera 'Palace Purple')
Plantain lily
(Hosta sieboldiana 'Elegans' and 'Sum and Substance')
Siberian iris
(Iris sibirica)
Herbaceous peonies
(Paeonia hybrids)
Russian sage
(Perovskia atriplicifolia)

Grasses & Ground Covers

Bearberry
(Arctostaphylos uva-ursi)
Sweet woodruff
(Galium odoratum)
Creeping Jenny
(Lysimachia nummularia)
Pachysandra
(Pachysandra terminalis)
Periwinkle
(Vinca minor)

Barrier & Screening

Anemone clematis
(Clematis montana)
Climbing hydrangea
(Hydrangea petiolaris)
Hardy climbing roses
(Rosa 'John Cabot' and 'Jens Monk')

Playhouse

Corrugated colored plastic   2×4 rafters

¾" painted plywood

2×6 bottom on concrete piers with ¾" plywood floor

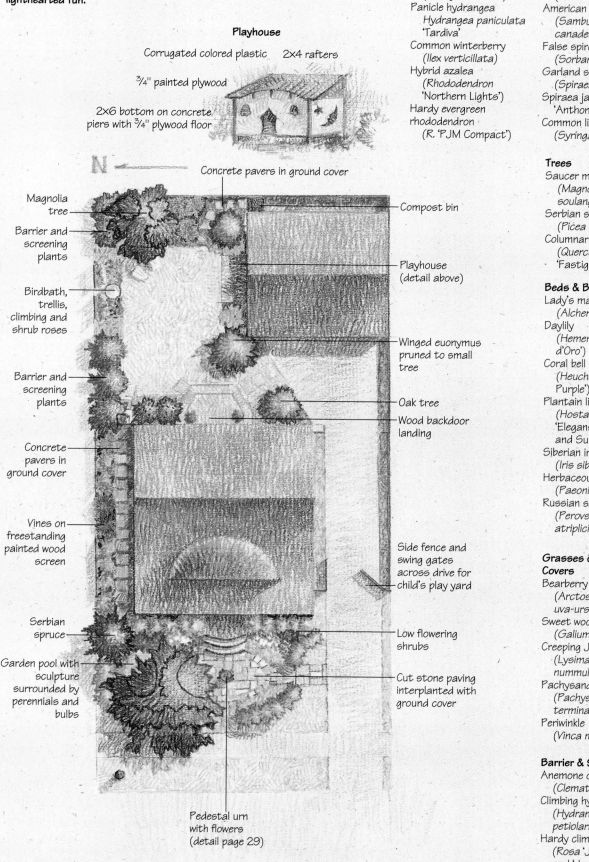

N

Concrete pavers in ground cover

Magnolia tree

Barrier and screening plants

Birdbath, trellis, climbing and shrub roses

Barrier and screening plants

Concrete pavers in ground cover

Vines on freestanding painted wood screen

Serbian spruce

Garden pool with sculpture surrounded by perennials and bulbs

Compost bin

Playhouse (detail above)

Winged euonymus pruned to small tree

Oak tree

Wood backdoor landing

Side fence and swing gates across drive for child's play yard

Low flowering shrubs

Cut stone paving interplanted with ground cover

Pedestal urn with flowers (detail page 29)

MONTREAL, QUEBEC, CANADA
RELAXATION AND WELCOME
by Audrey Day and Myke Hodgins, Landscape Architects, Montreal, Canada

Audrey Day and Myke Hodgins designed this plan for a single parent with elementary-school-age children. They saw their design task with dual goals—provide play spaces for the kids and give the adult an informal, inviting landscape with some areas for relaxation. The budget allowed $6,000 over two years, excluding the cost of a new play structure.

"The garden should be enjoyed as an extension of the inside," Myke says of their approach. "We often treat the yard as a series of rooms, creating identities specific to each."

To create a visually-compelling front yard, a garden with formal lines was planted with informal, easy-to-maintain plants that need no regular pruning. Spirea, peonies, hostas, and ground covers grow parterre-style, neatly arranged around a central entry court of cut stone. The play of colors and textures gives the small garden a charming presence. An urn planter on a pedestal in the center of the oval paving is a simple, yet elegant, focal point. Off to the left, a small water feature adds the sound of gentle splashing to set a relaxed and intimate mood. A path of concrete pavers along the north side leads through a shade garden to the backyard.

Wood screens along the pathway are cloaked with a mixture of clematis. The vines add privacy and interest with layers of foliage and flowers. Colorful shrubs and trees give the back perimeter garden a lush look. Climbing roses tumble over privacy screens. A curving lawn is the perfect spot for a play structure and children's activities. A whimsical playhouse, contracted for outside the landscape budget, was erected here adjacent to the garage and visible from the house. It is constructed of exterior-grade plywood sealed and painted bright colors with comical cutouts for windows. Its roof is made with panels of colored corrugated plastic.

Additional stones can be added by the owner to fashion a patio for entertaining and informal dining. Although native stone is used in many areas where it is plentiful and relatively inexpensive compared to the cost of poured concrete, a variety of aggregate-surfaced concrete pavers are universally available and economical.

Cut stone in the courtyard floor complements the facade of the residence (above). An antique planter urn is anchored into concrete for security (below).

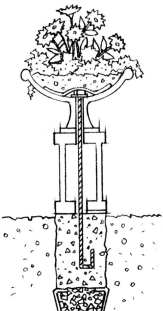

A new entry walk with flanking beds of color and
greenery welcomes visitors to the home's front door.

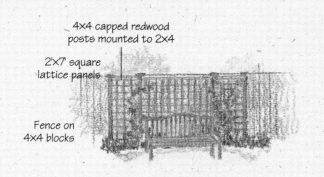

4×4 capped redwood
posts mounted to 2×4

2'×7 square
lattice panels

Fence on
4×4 blocks

Trees

Vine maple
    (Acer circinatum)
Red Japanese maple
    (A. palmatum
    'Atropurpureum')
Serviceberry
    (Amelanchier ×
    grandiflora 'Autumn
    Brilliance')
Chinese dogwood
    (Cornus kousa)

Witch hazel
    (Hamamelis mollis
    'Diane')
Magnolia
    (Magnolia stellata 'Royal
    Star')
Flowering cherry
    (Prunus × yedoensis
    'Akebono')

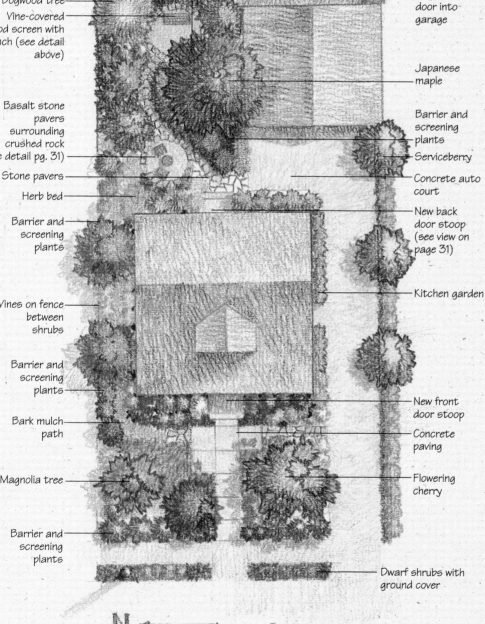

Garden pool under tree   Kiwi vines

Dogwood tree

Vine-covered
wood screen with
bench (see detail
above)

Basalt stone
pavers
surrounding
crushed rock
(see detail pg. 31)

Stone pavers

Herb bed

Barrier and
screening
plants

Vines on fence
between
shrubs

Barrier and
screening
plants

Bark mulch
path

Magnolia tree

Barrier and
screening
plants

Dog run with
door into
garage

Japanese
maple

Barrier and
screening
plants

Serviceberry

Concrete auto
court

New back
door stoop
(see view on
page 31)

Kitchen garden

New front
door stoop

Concrete
paving

Flowering
cherry

Dwarf shrubs with
ground cover

N

Shrubs

Enkianthus
    (Enkianthus campanulatus
    'Redvein')
Big-leaf hydrangea
    (Hydrangea macrophylla)
Drooping leucothoe
    (Leucothoe fontanesiana)
Heavenly bamboo
    (Nandina domestica)
Japanese pieris
    (Pieris japonica 'Valley Rose')
India hawthorn
    (Rhaphiolepis indica)
Azaleas and rhododendrons
    (Rhododendron hybrids)

Barrier & Screening

Five-leaf akebia
    (Akebia quinata)
Compact winged euonymus
    (Euonymus alata 'Compacta')
Hollyleaf osmanthus
    (Osmanthus ilicifolius)
English cherry laurel
    (Prunus laurocerasus 'Otto
    Luyken')
Box blueberry
    (Vaccinium ovatum)
Vaccinium ovatumiburnum
    (Viburnum davidiii)

Bedding & Borders

Sweet woodruff
    (Galium odoratum)
Blue hosta
    (Hosta sieboldiana)
Plantain lily
    (Hosta hybrids)
Sword fern
    (Polystichum munitum)

Grasses & Ground Covers

Japanese sedge
    (Carex morrowii 'Gold Band')
Variegated Japanese sedge
    (C. m. 'Variegata')
Drooping sedge
    (C. pendula)
Purple-leaf wintercreeper
    (Euonymus fortunei
    'Coloratus')
Japanese spurge
    (Pachysandra terminalis)
Periwinkle
    (Vinca minor 'Bowles')

Portland, Oregon
Nature and Convenience

by Julia Lundy, Landscape Architect, Julia Lundy Associates, P.C., Portland, Oregon

Transforming this midtown landscape into a functional and inspirational garden for a single professional woman who works at home was right up Julia Lundy's alley. She has designed many spaces on similar sites, although the $7,500 budget requires some do-it-yourself incentive from the client. "Security, privacy, and a fairly low-maintenance garden to putter in are the driving design considerations," Julia notes.

Cleaning up is the first step. Removing the large, unattractive tree that dominated the front yard and the overgrown mass of junipers along the foundation eliminates the unkempt look. This makes room for a new selection of colorful, low-maintenance shrubs, such as crimson pygmy barberry, purpleleaf wintercreeper, compact winged euonymus, and lingonberry. Careful attention to mature sizes helps prevent future security problems that can be caused by overgrown shrubbery. Native species included in the plant palette create a natural look and minimize yard chores. A few small trees add vertical interest to the composition.

Giving the small front yard a welcoming presence was a priority. Julia designed a new concrete walk and entry landing of generous proportions. This simple solution transforms the approach to the house and adds needed curb appeal.

The narrow bed on the south-facing side of the house is put to good use as a combination kitchen and flower garden. The size is perfect for someone who enjoys a little gardening but doesn't have time to maintain large, complicated planting beds. A screen of trees and shrubs along the driveway makes the garden area more intimate. An agreement with the south-side neighbor can lead to shared costs for this perimeter planting from which both homeowners might benefit.

Most of the design and materials budget was earmarked for the backyard. The design incorporates several benefits for frequent outdoor entertaining. A rapid-growing vine planted at the base of the fence will climb and cover it within a season. An added screen provides instant privacy to a new sitting area with a bench. Repeating the same vine to cloak the screen adds continuity to the landscape.

For guest parking, Julia added an auto court adjacent to and just west of the garage. Stone paving leads from the auto court to the home's rear entry. A new stoop and fresh plantings add appeal to the back door where visitors will often enter the home.

A new patio with a crushed stone floor is held in place with an edge of basalt stone pavers. It is tucked into a glen of native plantings on the north side of the rear garden. The inexpensive surfacing material keeps the project within budget and creates an attractive spot for relaxing or entertaining.

The rear garden beckons visitors into the landscape from indoors (above). The crushed stone patio (below) is contained with stone edging.

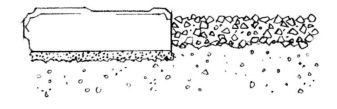

Front and rear areas of turf block paving create a novel solution for additional parking needs. A porte cochere (below, right) eliminates the tunnel effect of the long driveway.

Beds & Borders

False spiraea
(Astilbe spp.)
Sweet autumn clematis
(Clematis ternata)
Anemone clematis
(C. montana)
Peony
(Paeonia spp.)
Azalea
(Rhododendron hybrids)

Japanese wisteria
(Wisteria floribunda)
Bulbs
(Chionodoxa, Narcissus, Muscari, Scilla)
Grapes
Vegetables, herbs and annuals as available

Barrier & Screening

Common boxwood
(Buxus sempervirens 'Green Mountain')
Red-leaf Japanese barberry
(Berberis thunbergii 'Atropurpurea')
Inkberry
(Ilex glabra)
Juniper
(Juniperus virginiana 'Skyrocket')
Yew
(Taxus 'Nigra')

Grasses & Ground Covers

English ivy
(Hedera helix 'Thorndale')
Barren strawberry
(Waldsteinia fragarioides)

Trees

Assorted espaliered fruit trees for fences and walls

Ornamental pear for street trees
(Pyrus calleryana 'Redspire')

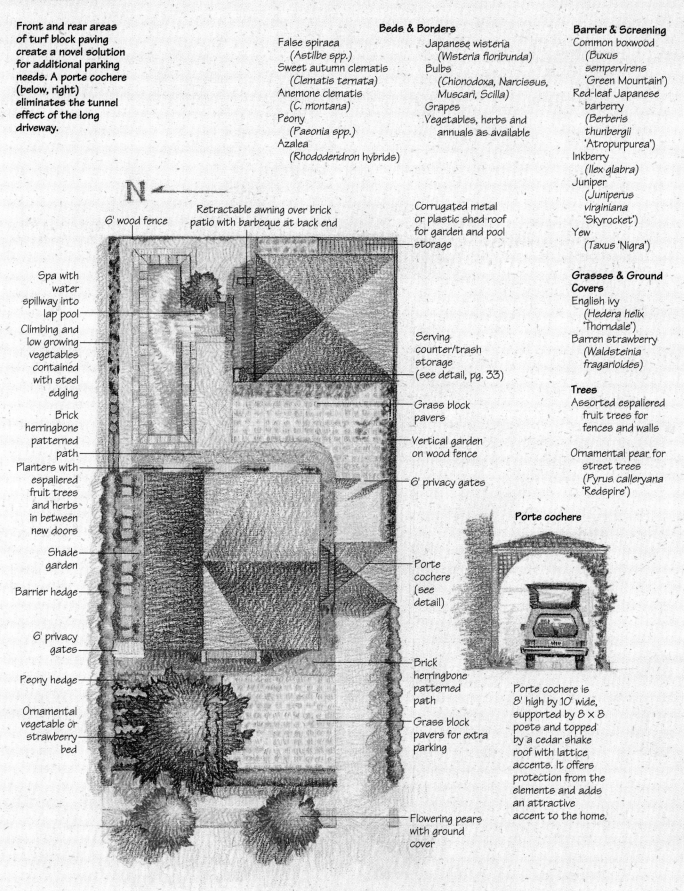

N

6' wood fence

Retractable awning over brick patio with barbeque at back end

Corrugated metal or plastic shed roof for garden and pool storage

Spa with water spillway into lap pool

Climbing and low growing vegetables contained with steel edging

Brick herringbone patterned path

Planters with espaliered fruit trees and herbs in between new doors

Shade garden

Barrier hedge

6' privacy gates

Peony hedge

Ornamental vegetable or strawberry bed

Serving counter/trash storage
(see detail, pg. 33)

Grass block pavers

Vertical garden on wood fence

6' privacy gates

Porte cochere
(see detail)

Brick herringbone patterned path

Grass block pavers for extra parking

Flowering pears with ground cover

Porte cochere

Porte cochere is 8' high by 10' wide, supported by 8 x 8 posts and topped by a cedar shake roof with lattice accents. It offers protection from the elements and adds an attractive accent to the home.

ST. LOUIS, MISSOURI
FUN AND GARDENING
by Kathy Williams, Landscape Architect, Williams and Associates, St. Louis, Missouri

Kathy Williams designed this total landscape renovation plan for a professional couple in their mid-fifties. The design offers opportunities for fresh-air entertaining and recreation. The budget of $8,500 does not include the lap pool and spa (they will be added separately, later).

"I feel the most important needs were achieving privacy, improving security, and finding space for off-street parking for guests," Kathy says of her design's priorities.

A portion of the front yard was converted into inconspicuous parking. Turf blocks add the support needed for two vehicles without the need for a hard, glaring surface. Meeting with the city to obtain permission to plant in the right-of-way was a worthwhile effort. The addition of a pair of street trees visually extends the yard, creating the illusion that the house is set farther back from the road.

A new vegetable garden takes advantage of the sunny western exposure. A paved entry area stretches across the width of the property, providing easy access along the home's facade. The paving links the driveway, front door, and vegetable garden. Perimeter hedges of upright juniper will grow quickly to form a privacy screen; they will double as a moderate noise barrier.

A new *porte cochere* built over the driveway gives the property an elegant touch. Flanking beds of flowering plants add color as they marry the new structure to the landscape. Wooden gates heighten security and modify the tunnel effect of the long driveway. A paved area along the north wall of the garage is sheltered by an awning. This transforms unused space into a pleasant place to relax beside the future pool and spa.

Kathy designed paving across the rear of the house with multiple access points to encourage an easy flow from indoors to out. Vertical plants growing in new planters are visible through windows from three rooms. This technique blurs the distinction between interior and exterior living spaces.

A 6-foot-high wooden fence replaces portions of the wire fence along the rear of the property. Vines grow on the existing fence along the northern boundary, providing privacy to a new kitchen garden. A stepping-stone path leads from the backyard to the front of the house through a richly textured shade garden of ivy, ferns, and bulbs.

Kathy notes that limestone flagstone could be used if it is more readily available in the area. Brick is a favorite among many designers and homeowners, although Kathy's experience has been that it gets too slippery when coated with moss in damp weather.

"A landscape, to be successful, should function for two or more purposes," Kathy observes. "This might include enhancement of the property as well as entertaining or some other outdoor activity."

A varied plant selection adds to the visual drama of the front landscape (above). Even a space for trash can add a touch of class with this well-designed enclosure (below).

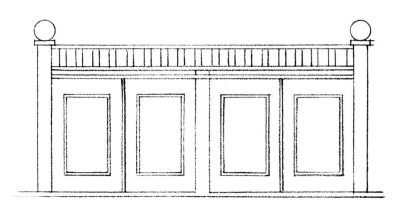

The large, pie-shaped lot calls for
privacy solutions and the creation
of usable outdoor spaces. The
awkward shape of the lot requires
creative design approaches to
develop a landscape that is both
attractive and functional.

SITE THREE: NEW SUBURBAN HOME ON CUL-DE-SAC

Like many new tract homes in suburbia, this 2,200 square foot split-level ranch is a good value for a young family. An investment now of time and money to establish a complementary landscape will increase the home's value as years pass.

The new house sits on a relatively level pie-shaped center lot at the end of a cul-de-sac. A broad driveway leads straight to a front garage. The lack of trees is typical of new construction. The terrain dips slightly in the back. Neighbors have erected a chain link fence along the eastern half of the rear lot line.

The kitchen, dining area, and living room are at street level with good access to the backyard. A master suite and two bedrooms are half a flight up; the family room, which opens onto the backyard, is half a flight down.

There are several site problems to address. The house seems plopped on its lot, with no transition from front yard to back and no connection between architecture and land. The entry to the house is poorly defined with nothing to direct attention to the front door area. The small front yard is dominated by double garage doors and an expansive driveway of glaring white concrete. The lack of trees means no shade and makes the height of the house seem imposing. The property consists of a single, impersonal exterior space. The large lawn is shapeless and takes a long time to mow. Multiple neighbors and no screening make the lack of privacy a top concern.

The designer has artfully shielded the home from public view by
layering shrubs and trees, developing inviting spaces for the
family without creating a "walled-in" feeling.

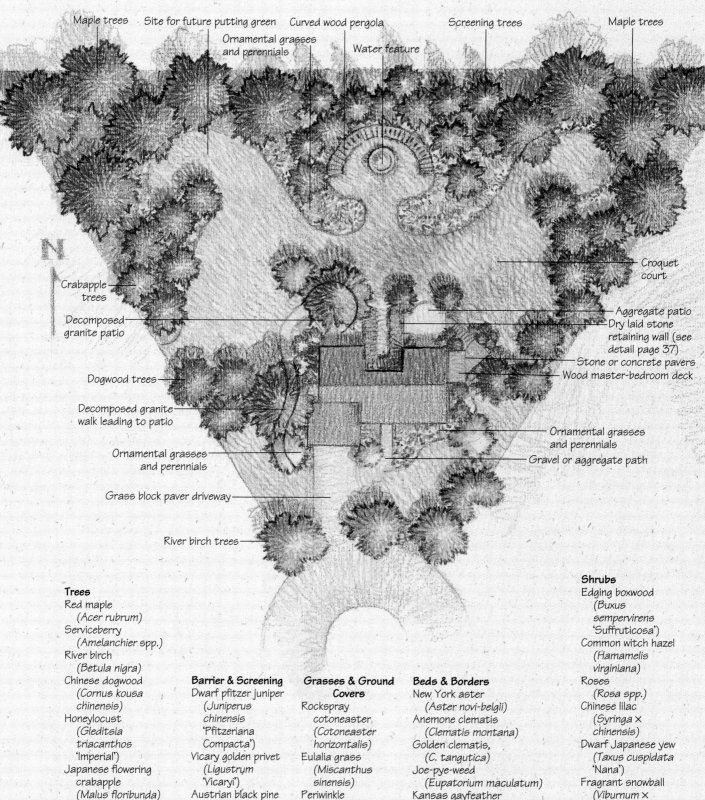

Maple trees   Site for future putting green   Curved wood pergola   Screening trees   Maple trees

Ornamental grasses and perennials   Water feature

N

Croquet court

Crabapple trees

Decomposed granite patio

Aggregate patio

Dry laid stone retaining wall (see detail page 37)

Stone or concrete pavers
Wood master-bedroom deck

Dogwood trees

Decomposed granite walk leading to patio

Ornamental grasses and perennials

Gravel or aggregate path

Ornamental grasses and perennials

Grass block paver driveway

River birch trees

Trees
Red maple
    (Acer rubrum)
Serviceberry
    (Amelanchier spp.)
River birch
    (Betula nigra)
Chinese dogwood
    (Cornus kousa
    chinensis)
Honeylocust
    (Gleditsia
    triacanthos
    'Imperial')
Japanese flowering
    crabapple
    (Malus floribunda)
Sargent crabapple
    (M. sargentii)
Bechtel crabapple
    (M. ioensis 'Plena')

Barrier & Screening
Dwarf pfitzer juniper
    (Juniperus
    chinensis
    'Pfitzeriana
    Compacta')
Vicary golden privet
    (Ligustrum
    'Vicaryi')
Austrian black pine
    (Pinus nigra)

**Grasses & Ground
Covers**
Rockspray
    cotoneaster
    (Cotoneaster
    horizontalis)
Eulalia grass
    (Miscanthus
    sinensis)
Periwinkle
    (Vinca minor)

Beds & Borders
New York aster
    (Aster novi-belgii)
Anemone clematis
    (Clematis montana)
Golden clematis,
    (C. tangutica)
Joe-pye-weed
    (Eupatorium maculatum)
Kansas gayfeather
    (Liatris pycnostachya)
Black-eyed Susan
    (Rudbeckia fulgida)
Goldenrod
    (Solidago)

Shrubs
Edging boxwood
    (Buxus
    sempervirens
    'Suffruticosa')
Common witch hazel
    (Hamamelis
    virginiana)
Roses
    (Rosa spp.)
Chinese lilac
    (Syringa ×
    chinensis)
Dwarf Japanese yew
    (Taxus cuspidata
    'Nana')
Fragrant snowball
    (Viburnum ×
    carlcephalum)
Weigela
    (Weigela spp.)

INDIANAPOLIS, INDIANA
BEAUTY AND FUN

by Ron Tisdale, Landscape Designer, R.L.Tisdale Co., Inc., Indianapolis, Indiana

A thirty-something couple with children in grade school would enjoy Ron Tisdale's easy-care and inviting landscape plan for this lot. Exterior views as well as views from within the home looking outward were important concerns. For first-time buyers on a limited budget, $15,000 to be spent over the course of 2 years is a significant amount for new home landscaping.

Ron began improvements by addressing the first impression of the property. A grove of river birch planted streetside attractively frames fragmented views of the house. Coarse-textured exfoliating bark, multiple trunks, leafy canopies, and a fast rate of growth makes these trees ideal for a big impact on curb appeal. Next, Ron removed the concrete driveway and replaced it with turf block pavers sown with grass seed for a less intrusive parking solution. A new pergola attached to the garage adds relief to the flat-fronted structure. Clematis planted at the foot of the pergola contributes the softening touch of foliage and flowers to the architecture.

Skirting the front lawn, a walkway of decomposed granite offers an attractive and inexpensive solution now that can be paved over later when funds permit. The new walk leads to the entry between a pair of witch hazels and past a foundation planting bed. Perennials and ornamental grasses make an immediate impact, adding color and texture to direct the path to the front door.

A new master bedroom deck commands a view of the east garden, where crabapples and red maples offer spring and fall color. Dogwood, viburnum, and fragrant lilac surround the deck and anchor the space.

A garden between the kitchen and master bedroom, glimpsed through a window wall in the living room, is a colorful mix of grasses, flowering shrubs, and perennials set between two fieldstone retaining walls. Austrian pine and crabapples form a background for a curved pergola with a central fountain. The location of these features is aligned with views from within the house.

A patio off the kitchen provides the family a place for fresh-air dining and relaxing. Connected to the front of the house by a curving path of decomposed granite, the patio is made of the same surface. This gives the large lot harmony and meets the budget.

The lawn, once an undefined expanse, now curves through the landscape. The shaped areas offer room for recreation and future amenities; the lawn functions as a lush, green rug in each outdoor room.

The inspiring view from the house (above) is toward the semicircular pergola and fountain across a luxurious swath of lawn. A cross section of the dry-laid stone retaining wall (left) shows plants growing in the cracks between stones.

This design divides the huge lot into manageable sections that minimize unused space. Instead of overwhelming the owners, the redesigned spaciousness is now appealing.

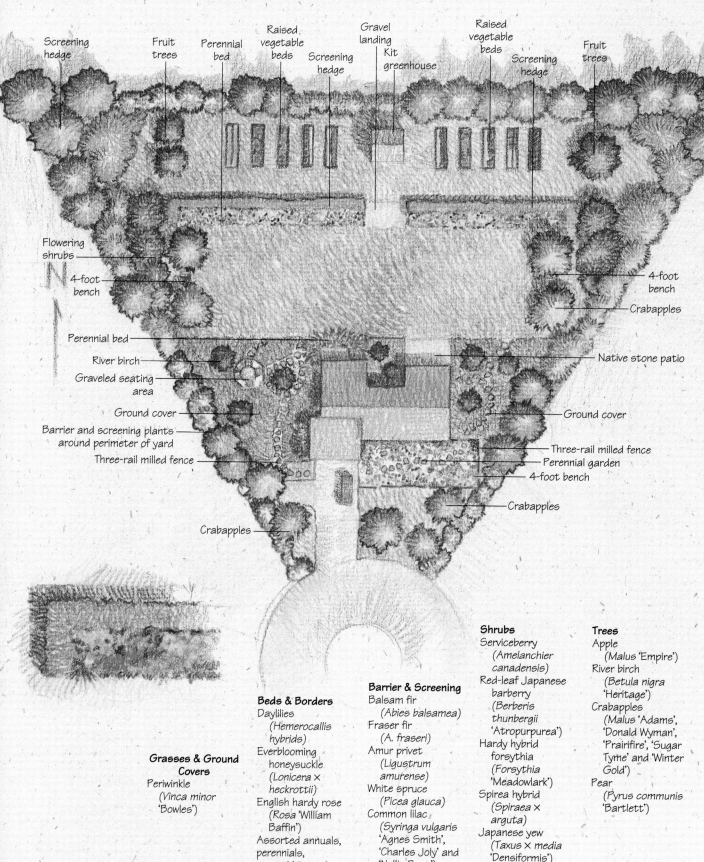

Screening hedge

Fruit trees

Perennial bed

Raised vegetable beds

Screening hedge

Gravel landing

Kit greenhouse

Raised vegetable beds

Screening hedge

Fruit trees

Flowering shrubs

4-foot bench

4-foot bench

Crabapples

Perennial bed

River birch

Native stone patio

Graveled seating area

Ground cover

Ground cover

Barrier and screening plants around perimeter of yard

Three-rail milled fence

Three-rail milled fence

Perennial garden

4-foot bench

Crabapples

Crabapples

Grasses & Ground Covers
Periwinkle (Vinca minor 'Bowles')

Beds & Borders
Daylilies (Hemerocallis hybrids)
Everblooming honeysuckle (Lonicera × heckrottii)
English hardy rose (Rosa 'William Baffin')
Assorted annuals, perennials, vegetables, and herbs as available

Barrier & Screening
Balsam fir (Abies balsamea)
Fraser fir (A. fraseri)
Amur privet (Ligustrum amurense)
White spruce (Picea glauca)
Common lilac (Syringa vulgaris 'Agnes Smith', 'Charles Joly' and 'Nellie Bean')

Shrubs
Serviceberry (Amelanchier canadensis)
Red-leaf Japanese barberry (Berberis thunbergii 'Atropurpurea')
Hardy hybrid forsythia (Forsythia 'Meadowlark')
Spirea hybrid (Spiraea × arguta)
Japanese yew (Taxus × media 'Densiformis')

Trees
Apple (Malus 'Empire')
River birch (Betula nigra 'Heritage')
Crabapples (Malus 'Adams', 'Donald Wyman', 'Prairifire', 'Sugar Tyme' and 'Winter Gold')
Pear (Pyrus communis 'Bartlett')

PUTNEY, VERMONT
RELAXATION AND GARDENING
by Gordon Hayward, Landscape Designer, Putney, Vermont

With retirement approaching, a couple in their mid-sixties would enjoy retiring to this attractive home and yard.

Hayward's landscape plan includes the beauty and bounty of a well-conceived garden. "I saw my task as setting the house into a garden without overwhelming the modest budget or the gardening skills of the owners," he says.

Spending $6,000 the first year and $3,000 the second, the plan solves problems and creates a pretty setting for enjoying time in the garden and the home.

Instead of going to the expense of remodeling, Gordon used artfully placed plant material to direct attention away from the large plane of paving and dominant garage doors. Crabapples and drifts of spirea give the front yard interest. The entry to the home, once bland and unimportant, is now delineated by a charming cottage garden. A gated fence surrounds the garden; visitors pass through this colorful and intimate space before entering the house. The defined area makes flower gardening an enjoyable— instead of overwhelming—prospect.

Stepping stone paths through vinca ground cover planted along both sides of the house lead to the back yard. Benches wait invitingly between crabapples at the eastern and western ends of an axial garden. Gordon chose these trees to provide beauty in spring, shade in summer, and interesting forms in winter when branches are bare.

Personal garden areas carved from the site make outdoor living appealing. A new dining area outside the kitchen is as comfortable as it is convenient. Limited access through master bedroom French doors makes this secret garden a true retreat.

Gordon's design celebrates the wide space of the pie-shaped lot. The lawn area behind the home is open and spacious. A gravel path leads to the rear of the property where two long perennial beds become a plentiful source of cut flowers. Above these beds, a fruit orchard offers the reward of harvest and screens an extensive vegetable garden. There's space in the center for a small greenhouse for the homeowners to shelter tender material in winter and propogate new plants. Balsam firs underplanted with colorful shrubs along the perimeter of the property offer screening for privacy and form backgrounds for carefully composed garden views.

The orchard, vegetable garden, and greenhouse are set against a screen of firs (above). An amure privet hedge and perennial beds shield this section of the landscape from direct public view.

A gravel path leads to the rear of the property (far left); stepping-stone paths set into vinca ground cover lead from front yard to back (center); a dropped edge border between lawn and perennial beds makes mowing easier (near left).

This ambitious design makes full use of the extensive property with access paths from the house that encircle the entire back yard. Usable amenities such as the built-in barbecue with tile counter and backsplash (detail below) are conveniently close to the house. Well-conceived front plantings minimize the dominance of the double garage doors.

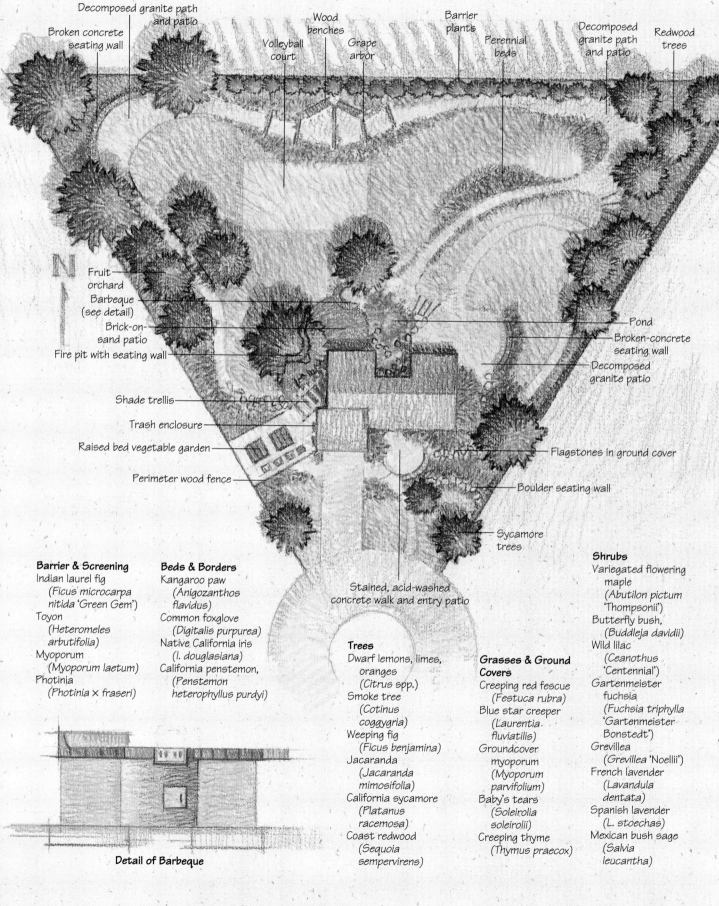

Decomposed granite path and patio

Broken concrete seating wall

Wood benches

Volleyball court

Grape arbor

Barrier plants

Perennial beds

Decomposed granite path and patio

Redwood trees

N

Fruit orchard

Barbeque (see detail)

Brick-on-sand patio

Fire pit with seating wall

Shade trellis

Trash enclosure

Raised bed vegetable garden

Perimeter wood fence

Pond

Broken-concrete seating wall

Decomposed granite patio

Flagstones in ground cover

Boulder seating wall

Sycamore trees

Stained, acid-washed concrete walk and entry patio

Detail of Barbeque

Barrier & Screening
Indian laurel fig
(Ficus microcarpa nitida 'Green Gem')
Toyon
(Heteromeles arbutifolia)
Myoporum
(Myoporum laetum)
Photinia
(Photinia × fraseri)

Beds & Borders
Kangaroo paw
(Anigozanthos flavidus)
Common foxglove
(Digitalis purpurea)
Native California iris
(I. douglasiana)
California penstemon,
(Penstemon heterophyllus purdyi)

Trees
Dwarf lemons, limes, oranges
(Citrus spp.)
Smoke tree
(Cotinus coggygria)
Weeping fig
(Ficus benjamina)
Jacaranda
(Jacaranda mimosifolia)
California sycamore
(Platanus racemosa)
Coast redwood
(Sequoia sempervirens)

Grasses & Ground Covers
Creeping red fescue
(Festuca rubra)
Blue star creeper
(Laurentia fluviatilis)
Groundcover myoporum
(Myoporum parvifolium)
Baby's tears
(Soleirolia soleirolii)
Creeping thyme
(Thymus praecox)

Shrubs
Variegated flowering maple
(Abutilon pictum 'Thompsonii')
Butterfly bush,
(Buddleja davidii)
Wild lilac
(Ceanothus 'Centennial')
Gartenmeister fuchsia
(Fuchsia triphylla 'Gartenmeister Bonstedt')
Grevillea
(Grevillea 'Noellii')
French lavender
(Lavandula dentata)
Spanish lavender
(L. stoechas)
Mexican bush sage
(Salvia leucantha)

TARZANA, CALIFORNIA
NATURE AND ENTERTAINING
by Nick Williams, Landscape Designer, Nick Williams & Associates, Tarzana, California

Nick Williams designed this landscape for a single parent whose teenage children visit on weekends and during summer vacation. The goal was to create a plan that emphasizes ecological awareness, contains several outdoor activity destinations, and adds charm to the home.

To stretch the budget—an allowance of $8,000 over a three-year period—the client planned to do some of the planting and construction work.

The ordinary entry was the first order of business. To minimize the visual impact of the oversized driveway and double-bay garage, Nick added a trellis above the garage doors for wisteria to weave its way across the face of the structure.

His design transforms the plain front yard into a garden filled with woodland plants. An entry walk of acid-washed concrete leads between a pair of planting beds and past a boulder seat wall to a generous landing of similarly treated concrete.

Sycamore trees provide shade in summer and balance the proportions of the story-and-a-half house on its lot. The canopy overhead makes the space comfortable for people walking through the landscape.

Flagstone paths on each side of the house lead to decomposed granite walkways that can be paved in the future. The master bedroom patio is also composed of decomposed gravel, an appropriate informal material for a garden beside a naturalistic pond.

Water plants and aquatic life create the intimacy of a little world. Stepping stones interplanted with baby tears, pennyroyal, and blue star creeper form a second seating area.

A Douglas fir arbor, stained to match the house and covered with lush climbers, offers welcome shade to the west-facing kitchen and dining room windows.

Nick designed a fire pit and seating wall for cool evenings beside the decomposed granite patio. Along the west wall of the garage, in an area screened by fencing, he planned a small kitchen garden and storage area with cabinets for trash and recyclables.

A small grove of citrus trees flanks a path winding along the western edge of the property. A surprise retreat in the far corner features a bench beneath a grape arbor.

A creeping red fescue lawn sown with California poppies and yarrow provides the center of the site with an open and sunny area, including room for a volleyball court.

Perimeter plantings of Ficus nitida, photinia, California sycamore, and coast redwood add privacy and claim the exterior space as part of the home.

The acid-washed patio, seating wall, lawn area, and stepping-stone path blend for inviting outdoor living (above). The overhead shade structure is constructed of Douglas fir, stained to blend with the house's finish.

The natural gas-powered fire pit (below) includes gas line and shut-off valve located by a seating wall.

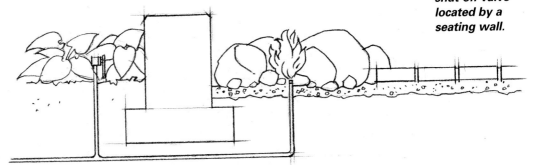

Inventive planting choices reduce the visual impact of double garage doors in this design. From a distance, the colorful azalea bed (far left) draws the eye away from the architecture. Closer in, a curved drive, enlarged entry and placement of specimen plants soften the view and create a welcoming atmosphere. Two drawings of the redwood entry pergola show both front and a side elevation (page 43).

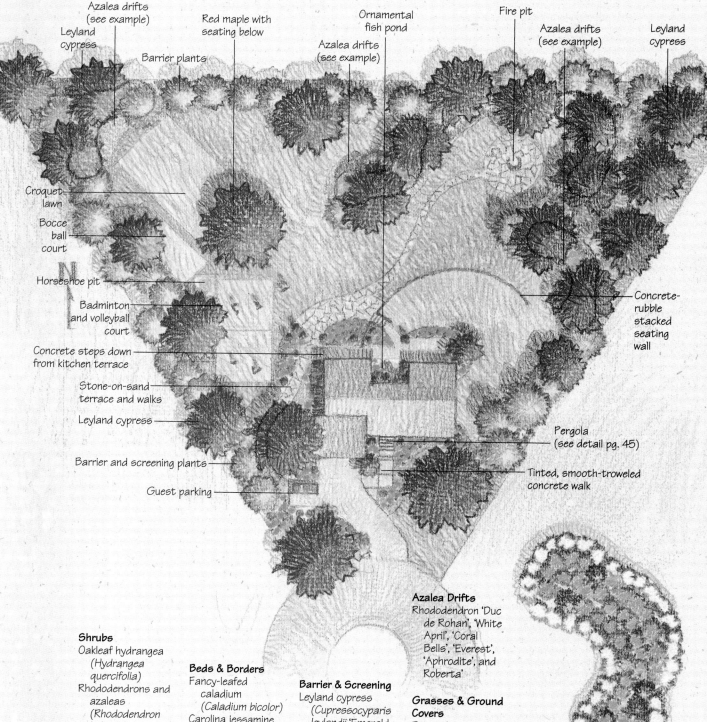

- Azalea drifts (see example)
- Leyland cypress
- Barrier plants
- Red maple with seating below
- Ornamental fish pond
- Azalea drifts (see example)
- Fire pit
- Azalea drifts (see example)
- Leyland cypress
- Croquet lawn
- Bocce ball court
- Horseshoe pit
- Badminton and volleyball court
- Concrete steps down from kitchen terrace
- Stone-on-sand terrace and walks
- Leyland cypress
- Barrier and screening plants
- Guest parking
- Concrete-rubble stacked seating wall
- Pergola (see detail pg. 45)
- Tinted, smooth-troweled concrete walk

Shrubs
Oakleaf hydrangea
    (Hydrangea
    quercifolia)
Rhododendrons and
    azaleas
    (Rhododendron
    hybrids)
Spiraea
    (Spiraea japonica
    'Albaflora' and
    'Alpina')
Doublefile viburnum
    (Viburnum
    plicatum
    tomentosum
    'Shasta')
Weigela
    (Weigela florida)

Beds & Borders
Fancy-leafed
    caladium
    (Caladium bicolor)
Carolina jessamine
    (Gelsemium
    sempervirens)
Christmas rose
    (Helleborus niger)
Plantain lily
    (Hosta varieties)
Big blue lily turf
    (Lirope muscari)
Mondo grass
    (Ophiopogon
    japonicus)

Barrier & Screening
Leyland cypress
    (Cupressocyparis
    leylandii 'Emerald
    Isle')
Silverberry
    (Elaeagnus
    pungens)
Yaupon holly
    (Ilex vomitoria)
Sweet mock orange,
    (Philadelphus
    coronarius)
Slash pine
    (Pinus elliottii)

Azalea Drifts
Rhododendron 'Duc
    de Rohan', 'White
    April', 'Coral
    Bells', 'Everest',
    'Aphrodite', and
    Roberta'

Grasses & Ground Covers
Bermudagrass
    (Cynodon
    dactylon
    'Tifgreen')
Tall fescue
    (Festuca
    arundinacea)
English ivy
    (Hedera helix
    'Needlepoint')
Dwarf periwinkle
    (Vinca minor)

Trees
Red maple
Sugar maple
River birch
Tulip poplar

DECATUR, ALABAMA
WELCOME AND CONVENIENCE
by Wilbur Abernethy, Landscape Architect, Decatur, Alabama

Wilbur Abernethy designed this open, friendly landscape for a professional couple with teenagers. It features as many outdoor features for adults and teens as an initial budget of $7,500 would allow. The plan offers informal and low-maintenance plantings, privacy from neighbors, and degrees of separation within the site for adults' and children's spaces.

In front, Wilbur realigned the driveway to reduce the visual impact of the runway-like paving and imposing garage doors. Planting heavily in front of the new curved driveway changed the focus of the approach to the house. A turnout added when the new drive was poured adds two guest parking spots.

The entry to the house gets dressed up with a walk composed of four large slabs of tinted concrete troweled smooth. The slabs join to form a path that turns a corner to connect parking areas with the front steps.

Colorful planting beds curve around the paving; the walkway guides guests through the plantings. A redwood pergola to the right adds an elegant note to the space.

Off the kitchen, a stone-on-sand terrace makes outdoor living easy and continues the curving, naturalistic theme. Irregularly shaped native limestone contributes an informal air.

A new fishpond nestled in an alcove can be seen from both the kitchen and the master bedroom, giving interior spaces an exterior focal point. This deliberate visual connection between indoors and out makes spaces flow together.

A retaining wall arcs behind the house, dividing the lawn space into levels and making the most of the view to landscaping at the lower end of the property. Careful planning yields separate outdoor rooms without sacrificing the spaciousness of the sight. This creates areas for teens and adults.

The northwest quadrant of the yard is devoted to recreation. A bocce ball court, croquet lawn, volleyball and badminton court, and a horseshoe pit are sited on a Bermuda lawn that can be converted to other uses after the kids have grown. Courts run roughly north to south to keep sun out of players' eyes.

From the kitchen terrace, a stone-on-sand path leads through the lawn to a patio with a central fire pit. This feature extends the season of exterior use and makes the patio a nighttime destination.

By locating this gathering area in the yard away from the house, Wilbur claimed more of the lot for active use. The relatively isolated location also contributes a campfire atmosphere.

A mixture of conifers and deciduous trees have a forest effect and provide essential privacy during the prime outdoor months. Curvilinear beds of colorful shrubs add another layer beneath trees and omit the need to mow around tree trunks.

Paths in the landscape lead to various outdoor amenities (above). These walkways are fieldstone set in a bed of sand and laid in curves for visual appeal. Front and side views of the pergola (below) show how it is constructed.

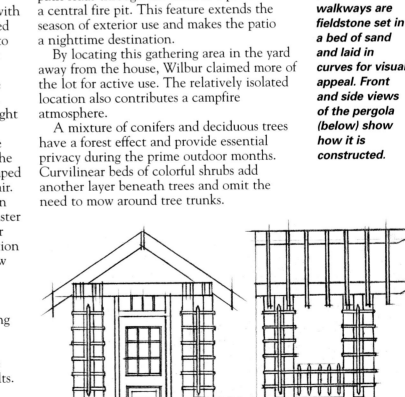

This dramatic slope
poses a challenge
for homeowners to
tame and reclaim.
An overall view of
the site shows how
the rock
outcroppings
intrude.

N

SITE FOUR: OLDER TOWNHOUSE ON STEEP CITY LOT

This older urban lot presents the challenge of a steep slope. No rear access for construction equipment makes landscaping this narrow property a difficult undertaking. A three-story townhouse occupies the front third of the 35-foot-wide, 130-foot-deep lot. There is virtually no front yard; two small planting pockets flank the garage. Two more areas of soil are squeezed between the public sidewalk and the curb. A utility pole is centered in one of these beds, dominating the area.

In the backyard, the terrain rises steeply from the house. The back property line is slightly higher than the third-floor sightline. A few scraggly trees and shrubs are scattered along the sloping site and across two large rock outcroppings, giving the area a desolate look.

Both the kitchen and dining room face the backyard and have access to it. Two bedrooms are located on the floor above.

The problems families face in urban settings are typical of this site. Giving the home personality is an important goal for the front yard. The small space must be improved to make it more inviting and distinctive.

In the backyard, adding much-needed privacy is a top priority. The difficult terrain must be reclaimed to maximize and enhance the small space. Relationships between the inside of the multistory home and its exterior space are nonexistent. No views or destinations compel people to venture outside. Drainage must be improved to move excess storm water and irrigation overflow out of the backyard.

Since the front of the landscape is virtually part of the public thoroughway, only minimal and durable plants are chosen. Most of the budget was used to transform the sloping site into a usable backyard. The rustic gazebo (top and side views, below) commands a view of the entire garden, and makes an intriguing destination.

Trees

Laceleaf Japanese maple
(*Acer palmatum dissectum* 'Atropurpureum')
European hornbeam
(*Carpinus betulus*)
Flowering dogwood
(*Cornus florida*)
Kousa dogwood
(*C. kousa*)
Carolina cherry laurel
(*Prunus caroliniana*)
Japanese snowbell
(*Styrax japonicus*)

Grasses & Ground Covers

Carpet bugle
(*Ajuga reptans* 'Burgundy Glow')
Barrenwort
(*Epimedium × youngianum* 'Niveum')
Sweet woodruff
(*Galium odoratum*)
Big blue lilyturf
(*Liriope muscari*)
Blue-flowered mazus
(*Mazus reptans*)
Periwinkle
(*Vinca minor*)

Barrier & Screening

American box
(*Buxus sempervirens*)
Leyland cypress
(× *Cupressocyparis leylandii*)
Foster's holly
(*Ilex × attenuata* 'Fosteri')
American holly
(*I. opaca*)

Beds & Borders

Goatsbeard
(*Aruncus dioicus*)
False spiraea
(*Astilbe* 'Deutschland')
Heartleaf bergenia
(*Bergenia cordifolia*)
Anemone clematis
(*C. montana* 'Reubens')
Cranesbill
(*Geranium* 'Johnson's Blue')
Hellebore
(*Helleborus foetidus*)
Plantain lily
(*Hosta* varieties)
Climbing hydrangea
(*Hydrangea anomala petiolaris*)

Siberian iris
(*Iris sibirica*)
Ostrich fern
(*Matteuccia struthiopteris*)
Maiden grass
(*Miscanthus sinensis* 'Gracillimus')
Fountain grass
(*Pennisetum alopecuroides* 'Hameln')
Russian sage
(*Perovskia ssp.*)
Sedum
(*Sedum* 'Autumn Joy')

Shrubs

Purple smokebush
(*Cotinus coggygria* 'Purpureus')
Witch hazel
(*Hamamelis × intermedia*)
Oakleaf hydrangea
(*Hydrangea quercifolia*)
Leatherleaf mahonia
(*Mahonia bealei*)
Heavenly bamboo
(*Nandina domestica*)

Rose
(*Rosa* 'The Fairy')
Rhododendrons and azaleas
(*Rhododendron* hybrids)
Spirea
(*Spiraea japonica* 'Goldflame')
Korean spice viburnum
(*Viburnum carlesii*)
Doublefile viburnum
(*V. plicatum tomentosum*)

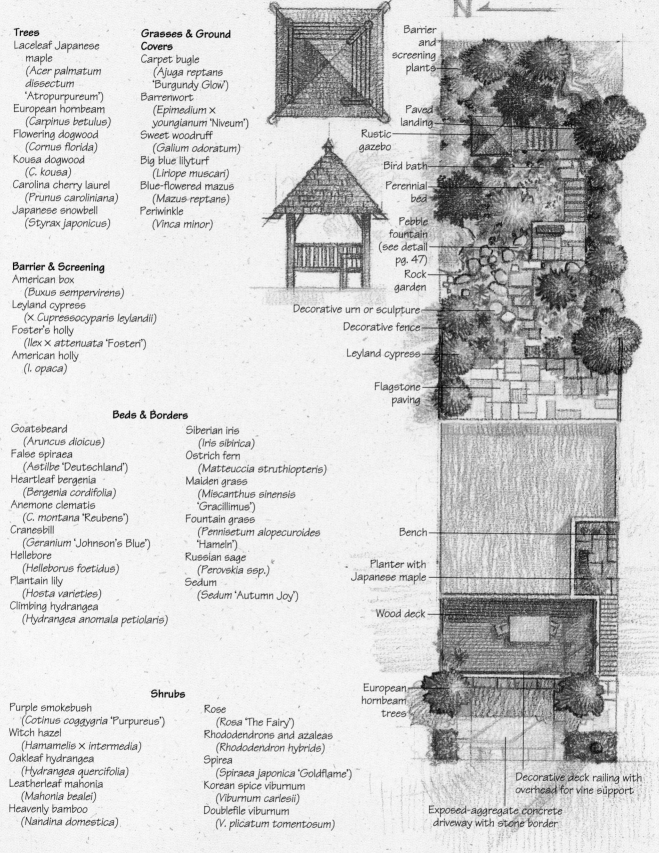

N

Barrier and screening plants
Paved landing
Rustic gazebo
Bird bath
Perennial bed
Pebble fountain (see detail pg. 47)
Rock garden
Decorative urn or sculpture
Decorative fence
Leyland cypress
Flagstone paving
Bench
Planter with Japanese maple
Wood deck
European hornbeam trees
Decorative deck railing with overhead for vine support
Exposed-aggregate concrete driveway with stone border

WASHINGTON, D. C.
BEAUTY AND RELAXATION

by Joanne Lawson, Landscape Architect, Lawson Carter Epstein, Washington, D.C.

Tightly packed townhomes are commonplace in the Washington, D.C., area, so Joanne Lawson was not daunted by this challenge. She designed this plan for a mid-thirties couple who would install the backyard garden themselves, containing costs on the somewhat restrictive $15,000 budget. The plan also rehabilitates the front yard to make it more appealing.

Because most of the budget would need to be spent in the back, a simple yet elegant solution in the front was to pave a new driveway with exposed aggregate surrounded by a 24-inch flagstone border.

A European hornbeam underplanted with liriope in each of the two beds flanking the drive are a simple combination for the small space. The vertical form of these trees has a sophisticated air and complements the three-story home.

For the entry, Joanne designed a flagstone patio with a bench and large planter housing a weeping Japanese maple. Adding a containerized tree makes a dramatic accent, featuring fine-textured foliage most of the year and a sculptural form in winter months.

In the backyard, the flagstone paving is repeated in a lower terrace that is concealed by decorative screens. A flight of steps with wooden risers and stone treads winds its way past a rock garden where a simple fountain bubbles like a spring over river stones.

Lush plantings curve upward to another landing. There, a bench is perfect for admiring the view. Stairs continue uphill to a final landing below a rock outcropping.

A new rock garden is at home in this location. Dense planting of woodland shrubs around a birdbath complements the natural scheme and provides cover for songbirds, attracting them to the backyard.

Joanne designed a rustic gazebo that commands a view of the entire garden. Set among plantings of Leyland cypress, American holly, and doublefile viburnum for maximum privacy and solitude, the gazebo can be glimpsed from within the garden, making it a tantalizing destination worth climbing steps to reach.

The rear garden is an attractive series of ascending landings (above).

A ½-horsepower recirculating pump is the hidden source driving the water feature (below).

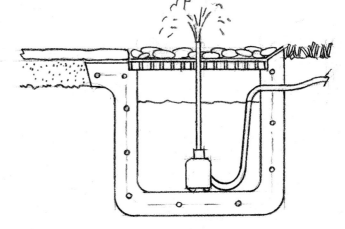

Beds & Borders

Maidenhair fern
(*Adiantum pedatum*)
Wild columbine
(*Aquilegia canadensis*)
Jack-in-the-pulpit
(*Arisaema triphyllum*)
Wild ginger
(*Asarum canadense*)
Butterfly weed
(*Asclepias tuberosa*)
Big-leaf aster
(*A. macrophyllus*)
Blue false indigo
(*Baptisia australis*)
Harebell
(*Campanula rotundifolia*)
Black cohosh or snakeroot
(*Cimicifuga racemosa*)
Shooting star
(*Dodecatheon meadia*)
Wild cranesbill
(*Geranium maculatum*)
Dwarf crested iris
(*Iris cristata*)
Button blazing star
(*Liatris aspera*)
Ostrich fern
(*Matteuccia
struthiopteris*)
Virginia bluebells
(*Mertensia virginica*)
Interrupted fern
(*Osmunda claytoniana*)
Switchgrass
(*Panicum virgatum*)

Foxglove penstemon
(*Penstemon digitalis*)
Slender penstemon
(*Penstemon gracillus*)
Wild sweet William
(*Phlox divaricata laphamii*)
Creeping phlox
(*P. stolonifera 'Blue Ridge'*)
Solomon's seal
(*Polygonatum
commutatum*)
Christmas fern
(*Polystichum
acrostichoides*)
Pasque flower
(*Pulsatilla patens*)
Prairie coneflower
(*Ratibida pinnata*)
Black-eyed Susan
(*Rudbeckia hirta*)
Cup plant
(*Silphium perfoliatum*)
Showy goldenrod
(*S. speciosa*)
Foamflower
(*Tiarella cordifolia*)
Culver's root
(*Veronicastrum virginicum*)
Little bluestem
(*Schizachyrium scoparium*)
Indian grass
(*Sorghastrum nutans*)
Prairie dropseed
(*Sporobolus heterolepis*)

Trees
Saskatoon
(*Amelanchier alnifolia*)
Crabapple
(*Malus 'Donald Wyman'*)
Quaking aspen
(*Populus tremuloides*)

Shrubs
Serviceberry
(*Amelanchier spp.*)
Japanese barberry
(*Berberis thunbergii*)
Forsythia
(*Forsythia spp.*)
Spirea
(*Spiraea spp.*)
Lilac
(*Syringa spp.*)

Barrier & Screening
Eastern red cedar
(*Juniperus virginiana*)
Trumpet honeysuckle
(*Lonicera sempervirens*)
Virginia creeper
(*Parthenocissus quinquefolia*)

A front elevation shows the pergola and rail details over garage (below); since there is no front space, a deck over the garage provides outdoor access in comfort and privacy. A bird's-eye view of the entire property illustrates how the steep slope was conquered with steps and switchbacks.

Barrier and screening plants

Rock side walls

Fieldstone terrace

Gravel or crushed rock path with railroad tie steps

Prairie plantings

Goldfish pond

Wood trellis

Concrete terrace

Shade garden

Shallow pool with spillway (see detail pg. 49)

Crab apple

Deck with pergola

Wood planter boxes with colorful annuals or perennials

Plantings of vines and prairie grasses

Little bluestem beds

N ←

Vine trellis and prairie-style deck railing (see detail)

MINNEAPOLIS, MINNESOTA
NATURE AND WELCOME

by Colston Burrell, Landscape Designer,
Native Landscape Design & Restoration
Ltd., Minneapolis, Minnesota

This Upper Midwest landscape interpretation was designed with a couple in their fifties in mind. Their children grown and gone, this couple would select the townhouse for their empty nest. The larger budget of $25,000 allows them to hire more of the work done to create this naturalistic garden on the steep site, including amenities for enjoying the wonders of nature, such as bird-watching.

Colston Burrell enjoys designing naturalistic landscapes. He set the theme for this garden by planting little bluestem, a handsome ornamental grass, in the front beds. A rooftop pergola with prairie-style rails is situated above the garage and festooned with vines for shade from hot sun from the west and south. The design is eye-catching and virtually maintenance-free.

Over a new terrace shared by the dining room and kitchen, another vine-covered arbor adds privacy. This previously unused area is transformed into a favorite destination. Ferns and shade plants border both ends of the paving. Water features add a touch of life along the eastern edge of the terrace. A goldfish pond is built to resemble a natural pool, with moving water spilling over and collecting in a shallow pool to attract birds and butterflies. The sound of water enhances the secluded feeling.

A short flight of stairs up the slope leads to a garden of prairie plants. Opposite this area, a grove of eastern red cedar and saskatoon continues the native theme and adds privacy. A fieldstone terrace sits a few steps higher. Continued steps, always interrupted by landings to keep the trail unintimidating, curve around more prairie plantings and trees higher on the site. No mowing is ever needed.

A final switchback leads to the summit, where a fieldstone terrace blends almost seamlessly into the massive rock outcropping at the top of the property. Planting a backdrop of conifers and deciduous trees suggests a forest. Red cedar stays green year-round, setting off the colorful foliage and

stark trunks of quaking aspen, while saskatoon lures birds to this backyard oasis.

All the rock walls Colston designed utilize large, irregularly shaped material to mirror the natural rock outcroppings on the site.

"The steps appear to be carved from the native rock," Colston explains. Native prairie perennials and grasses continue the naturalistic setting provided by this plan.

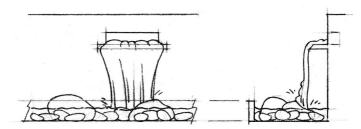

A detail of the spillway-and-pool water feature.

The designer's solution to a knotty landscape problem: Terracing creates rooms on different levels in back for entertaining and enjoying the outdoors. A large, permanent buffet table on the lower terrace makes dining outside an easy option (detail, below).

Trees
Japanese maple
  (Acer palmatum)
Laceleaf Japanese maple
  (A. p. dissectum)
Pacific dogwood
  (Cornus nuttallii)
Bronze loquat
  (Eriobotrya deflexa)
Colorado blue spruce
  (Picea pungens 'Glauca')
Chinese elm
  (Ulmus parvifolia)

Shrubs
California allspice
  (Calycanthus occidentalis)
Spreading coprosma
  (Coprosma × kirkii)
Sun rose
  (Helianthemum nummularium)
Weeping lantana
  (Lantana montevidensis)
Rosemary
  (Rosmarinus officinalis)
Germander
  (Teucrium chamaedrys)

Beds & Borders
Dwarf lily-of-the-nile
  (Agapanthus 'Peter Pan')
Cranesbill
  (Geranium spp.)
Daylily
  (Hemerocallis 'Stella d'Oro')
Virginia creeper
  (Parthenocissus quinquefolia)
Ivy geranium
  (Pelargonium peltatum)
Dwarf New Zealand flax
  (Phormium tenax 'Bronze Baby')
Western sword fern
  (Polystichum munitum)
Chinese wisteria
  (Wisteria sinensis)
Spanish dagger
  (Yucca gloriosa)
Ornamental grasses of your choice

Barrier & Screening
Toyon
  (Heteromeles arbutifolia)
California wax myrtle
  (Myrica californica)
Tobira
  (Pittosporum tobira)

Grasses & Ground Covers
English ivy
  (Hedera helix)
Mondo grass
  (Ophiopogon japonicus)

Japanese maples

Wood deck

Railroad tie steps

Spruce in fern and ground cover bed

Urn with perennials

Perennial bed

Dry-laid concrete-rubble retaining wall

Barrier and screening plants

Shrub and ground cover bed
Wall-mounted fountain

Wood retaining wall and wood seating wall (see detail, pg. 51)

Chinese elm

Japanese maples with mondo grass and wall ivy

Brick-on-sand terrace

Storage shed with decorative doors

Display/serving table with wisteria-covered columned trellis

Matching decorative doors mounted on wood fence

Three wood and canvas screens

Vine-covered wall

Cedar decking

New scored and patterned drive and sidewalk

Loquat street trees with ground cover

N

SAN FRANCISCO, CALIFORNIA
ENTERTAINING AND CONVENIENCE
by Emery Rogers, Emery Rogers and Associates, San Francisco, California

The plan prepared for this lot with its neglected and virtually useless backyard was designed with a single professional and one teenager in mind. Emery Roger's firm has transformed the challenging topography into accessible and useful space on a $25,000 budget.

Because the front beds are exposed to much pedestrian traffic, only minimal planting works. Four bronze loquats, one in each planting area, supply vertical definition to the previously flat area. Underplanting each tree with ground cover eliminates the need to get the mower out for such small areas. This durable type of plant suits the public location. Using only two species of plants in the front yard creates identity and unity to what was small, uninteresting space.

Saw-cutting new score lines enhances the driveway and entry walk inexpensively. The resulting grid pattern aligns with the trees for a formal, symmetrical look.

The backyard needed privacy, space for entertaining, and a solution for the slope. "In the rear yard, we wanted to avoid high retaining walls, so we divided the entertaining terraces into two levels," Emery notes. "These levels can accommodate several tables."

He designed a large, permanent buffet table on the lower terrace, making dining outside an easy option. The buffet doubles as a display surface for potted plants and garden sculpture. Instead of installing a permanent barbeque, the homeowner selected a portable cooker to stow out of sight when not in use.

Steps lead to the upper terrace, made of brick-on-sand. Because this construction requires no concrete or mortar, materials can be brought in by wheelbarrow to the restricted site. A wood retaining wall adds privacy to this outdoor room, accommodating gatherings that flow from house to yard.

A second flight of stairs leads up to another room with a lawn, providing transition from the hard surfaces below. A fieldstone retaining wall with a decorative urn in the center adds a note of elegance to this space.

Curved steps allow access to the top elevation of the garden, where a wooden deck is surrounded by a grove of Japanese maples. Future plans call for enclosing the deck with screened walls and adding an overhead structure for use during inclement weather.

For privacy screening, layers of evergreen and deciduous shrubs and trees have been carefully placed to provide maximum seclusion.

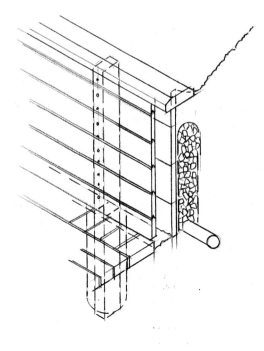

A schematic of the wooden retaining wall used to subdue the rear slope. The wall is covered with T&G shiplapped siding and capped with cedar.

An overhead perspective of the property illustrates the terracing techniques. The detail (below) shows the nature-trail step system developed with crushed rock and railroad ties.

Barrier & Screening
Variegated Japanese privet,
    (Ligustrum japonicum 'Silver Star')

Grasses & Ground Covers
Blue fescue
    (Festuca ovina glauca)
Marathon II Improved grass,
    (sod or seed)
Spreading verbena
    (Verbena peruviana)

Shrubs
Dwarf Japanese boxwood
    (Buxus microphylla
    japonica 'Compacta')
Wild lilac
    (Ceanothus griseus
    horizontalis)
French lavender
    (Lavandula dentata)
Roses
    (Rosa spp.)

Cleveland sage,
    (Salvia clevelandii)
Mexican bush sage
    (S. leucantha)
Lavender cotton
    (Santolina
    chamaecyparissus)

Trees
Blue Italian cypress
    (Cupressus sempervirens
    'Glauca')
Dwarf blood orange
    (Citrus sinensis 'Moro')
Dwarf Nagami kumquat
    (Fortunella margarita)
Dwarf lemon
    (C. limon 'Sungold')

Dwarf Algerian tangerine
    (C. reticulata 'Clementine')
Crape myrtle
    (Lagerstroemia indica
    'Natchez' and 'Muskogee')
Western tea myrtle
    (Melaleuca nesophila)
Olive (no fruit or pollen)
    (Olea europaea 'Swan Hill')

Beds & Borders
Cape mallow
    (Anisodontea
    hypmandarum 'Tara's Pink')
Tree mallow
    (Lavatera assurgentiflora)
Dwarf pittosporum
    (Pittosporum crassifolium
    'Compactum')
Rose
    (Rosa floribunda 'Iceberg')
Trailing rosemary
    (Rosmarinus officinalis
    'Prostratus')

Upright rosemary
    (R. o. 'Tuscan Blue')
Lilac sage
    (Salvia verticillata)
Dwarf lavender cotton
    (Santolina
    chamaecyparissus 'Nana')
Dwarf santolina
    (S. ericoides 'Lemon Queen')
Herbs and vegetables as
    available

Nature trail of crushed rock with railroad-tie steps (see detail)

Fort playhouse on lawn (see detail pg.53)

4 Olive trees

Railroad-tie retaining wall

Herb garden

Vegetable garden

Rock garden

Arbor with stone in sand patio

Low hedge

Rose garden

Railroad tie retaining wall and steps

Italian cypress

Wall fountain on retaining wall

Random stone on concrete

Crape myrtle

Perimeter of flowering shrub and perennial beds

Wood decking

4 Citrus trees

Pots of lavender with blue fescue

Crape myrtle underplanted with flowering shrubs and ground cover

Random-stone driveway and entry walk

CORONA DEL MAR, CALIFORNIA
FUN AND GARDENING
by Greg Grisamore, Landscape Designer, Greg Grisamore & Associates, Corona del Mar, California

Greg Grisamore designed this plan for a couple with two elementary-school-age boys, who would want such a townhouse for its convenient proximity to the city. Salvaging livable outdoor space from the steeply sloping back yard on a budget of $25,000 is a challenge.

"This yard presents some of the most challenging topography a designer can work with," Greg recalls. "Because of the steepness of the lot, adding terraces is the only way to add access."

He started by designing a new look for the flat front yard. To create a more inviting entry, Greg suggested cut stone be laid over the driveway and extended to make an entry walk. A crape myrtle and iceberg roses with a blue fescue border were planted in each small planting pocket.

Next, Greg designed a rooftop deck above the garage for casual meals, entertaining, and relaxation. Large citrus trees growing in oversized terra-cotta pots underplanted with green santolina and upright rosemary anchor deck corners with color and texture.

Terraces are the answer to taming the steep backyard slope. Random-laid stone paving is easily mortared in place atop an existing concrete slab, creating a more finished look. White-blooming Natchez crape myrtles grow quickly, adding height, shade, sculptural trunks, and summer flowers. Greg's design repeats crape myrtles at the corners and defines the space with a boxwood hedge. A wall fountain serves as the focal point of this pleasant and easily accessible outdoor room.

Railroad tie steps lead to a second-level terrace. The random-size stone set in a sand base forms an octagon, which is repeated in the design of an irresistible play structure. Four corner niche gardens dominate this level. A lawn play space, a pocket vegetable garden, an herb garden, and roses flourish in the formerly barren backyard.

A final flight of railroad tie steps leads to a nature trail sheltered by a grove of melaleuca trees along the upper portion of the lot.

"With a project of this type where steep, sloping terrain is involved, it is crucial to solve drainage and erosion problems at the outset," Greg comments. "Once seasonal rains begin to nibble away at the soil on hills, it's too late."

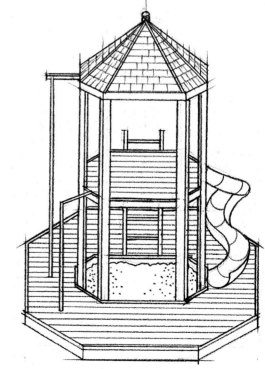

Schematic of a two-story play fort with slide, ropes, and sandbox, located on a rear terrace (Design by Michael Glassman & Associates)

An overhead perspective of the site shows the small plot of land
the designers will work with. Most approaches will involve scaled-
down versions of typical amenities, such as a spa or lap pool
instead of a conventional pool, or a small patio in lieu of a deck.
Since every detail is close to view, all ingredients will need to work
harmoniously together.

N

SITE FIVE: NEW CONDO, END LOT

This plan is typical of townhomes and condominiums coast to coast. It is a two-story end unit on a small lot. The living and dining areas are downstairs, adjacent to the kitchen. Bedrooms are on the upper floor.

In recent years, condominium living has become the favored option for many first-time buyers, such as young families with small budgets just starting out. An older generation favors these homes, too, as empty nesters and retirees look for smaller accommodations with little or no outdoor maintenance.

The lot is 75 feet deep and 40 feet wide. There's a front court that is 15 feet deep and 20 feet wide, a 6-foot-wide side yard, and a small backyard with some view. The regularity of exterior spaces and the similarity of architecture within the development leave houses unidentifiable and impersonal on the outside.

Other problems common to this type of home include a lack of privacy, inadequate room for many outdoor amenities, and a lack of connection between the interior floor plan and the outdoor spaces. Designing improvements is tricky, as care must be taken not to clutter the small space with complicated schemes. There are rarely any existing trees of significant size on the lots, as construction of the units usually eliminates most trees within a certain range of the foundation. Most condominium associations provide perimeter fencing; some prohibit owners from changing the exterior appearance of such enclosures or extending heights.

N

Two perspectives of this Southwest landscape: A bird's-eye view shows the entire plan (this page), while a front elevation illustrates the use of pots of greenery and the privacy wall (detail below). The lattice ramada (page 57) provides dappled shade.

Shrubs

Stepping stones in crushed granite

Vines along back wall

Berm with shrubs and native boulders

Cat's-claw vine on 6' stucco kitchen wall

Ground cover, perennials and low shrubs

Pond

Weeping pittosporum trees

Basketweave brick entry

Cactus or low-maintenance perennials in pots

Banco (seating wall)

5' high stucco privacy wall

Wood-trellised ramada (see detail page 57)

Barbeque

Flagstone patio

Drought tolerant tree with stepping stones in crushed granite underneath

Courtyard dining patio

Beds & Borders

Peruvian cactus
  (*Cereus peruvianus*)
Fortnight lily
  (*Dietes vegeta*)
Dahlberg daisy
  (*Thymophylla tenuiloba*)
Geranium
  (*Pelargonium spp.*)

Desert beard tongue
  (*Penstemon pseudospectabilis*)
Matilija poppy
  (*Romneya coulteri*)
Lemon marigold
  (*Tagetes lemmonii*)

Barrier & Screening

Cat's-claw vine
  (*Macfadyena unguis-cati*)
Asiatic jasmine
  (*Trachelospermum asiaticum*)
Star jasmine
  (*T. jasminoides*)
Snail flower
  (*Vigna caracalla*)

Trees

Mexican palo verde
  (*Parkinsonia aculeata*)
Fraser photinia
  (*Photinia × fraseri*)
Willow pittosporum
  (*Pittosporum phillyraeoides*)
Chaste tree
  (*Vitex agnus-castus*)

Grasses & Ground Covers

Silver artemesia
  (*Artemisia schmidtiana* 'Silver Mound')
Ground morning glory
  (*Convolvulus mauritanicus*)
Sweet alyssum
  (*Lobularia maritima* 'Carpet of Snow')
White evening primrose
  (*Oenothera caespitosa*)
Tifgreen turfgrass

Shrubs

Dwarf heavenly bamboo
  (*Nandina domestica* 'Compacta')
Dwarf oleander
  (*Nerium oleander* 'Petite Pink')
Philodendron
  (*Philodendron selloum* 'Lundii')
Dwarf India hawthorn
  (*Rhaphiolepis indica* 'Ballerina')
Lavender cotton
  (*Santolina chamaecyparissus*)

TUCSON, ARIZONA
BEAUTY AND WELCOME
by Mary Rose Duffield, Landscape Designer, Tucson, Arizona

Mary Rose Duffield designed this plan for a couple in their early sixties purchasing this condominum for a retirement home where they can enjoy socializing with resident friends. The hot summer climate of their region and a desire for limited outdoor chores made an attractive, low-maintenance entry and entertainment spaces the top priorities.

Mary Rose designed the new front entry to reflect the evolving blend of traditions of several cultures that have settled in the area.

Containers are set on an entry *banco,* a Spanish masonry bench stuccoed to blend with the exterior. Other potted plants decorate the top of a new privacy wall. "Containers are the item of choice for color and cactus, and I used these as welcoming accents at the front," Mary Rose comments.

The new wall shields a dining patio from view, making it a favorite spot. The warm red hue of brick-on-sand laid in a basketweave pattern echoes the color of roof tiles.

In the backyard, a flagstone patio with a built-in grill provides space for entertaining. A pond with a fountain provides a hint of coolness with the soothing sound of moving water. The fresh green of a small lawn beyond the patio complements the cooling scheme.

Easy-to-grow photinia, monk's pepper, weeping pittosporum, and Indian hawthorn grow around the perimeter, enhancing privacy. A lattice-roofed ramada over the patio offers dappled shade for a pleasant place to sit and enjoy the garden.

A cookout center sheltered by a lattice-covered ramada (above) is the focal point of this flagstone patio, which commands a view of the entire garden. Details (left) show the ramada construction.

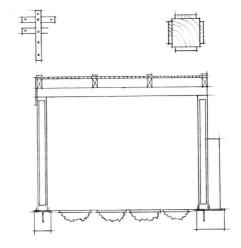

A fenced courtyard adds elegance to this landscape design. The wall trellis at the rear entry (detail, below) makes it possible to repeat bright flowers from the garden.

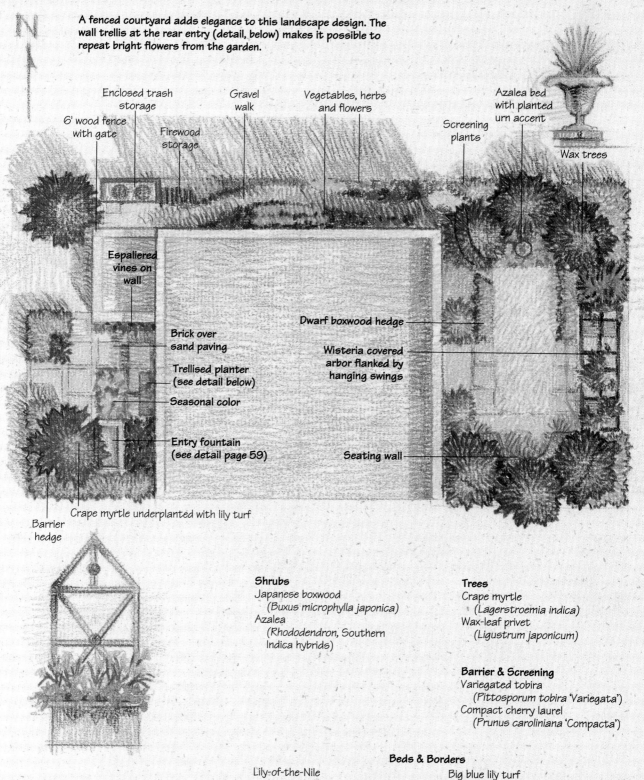

N

Enclosed trash storage

6' wood fence with gate

Firewood storage

Gravel walk

Vegetables, herbs and flowers

Screening plants

Azalea bed with planted urn accent

Wax trees

Espaliered vines on wall

Brick over sand paving

Trellised planter (see detail below)

Seasonal color

Entry fountain (see detail page 59)

Dwarf boxwood hedge

Wisteria covered arbor flanked by hanging swings

Seating wall

Barrier hedge

Crape myrtle underplanted with lily turf

Shrubs
Japanese boxwood
(*Buxus microphylla japonica*)
Azalea
(*Rhododendron*, Southern Indica hybrids)

Trees
Crape myrtle
(*Lagerstroemia indica*)
Wax-leaf privet
(*Ligustrum japonicum*)

Barrier & Screening
Variegated tobira
(*Pittosporum tobira* 'Variegata')
Compact cherry laurel
(*Prunus caroliniana* 'Compacta')

Beds & Borders
Lily-of-the-Nile
(*Agapanthus africanus*)
Foxtail fern
(*Asparagus densiflorus* 'Myers')
Rieger begonia
(*Begonia × hiemalis*)
Strapleaf caladium
(*Caladium bicolor*)
Cyclamen
(*Cyclamen hederifolium*)
Holly fern
(*Cyrtomium falcatum*)

Big blue lily turf
(*Liriope muscari*)
Star jasmine
(*Trachelospermum jasminoides*)
Pansy
(*Viola × wittrockiana*)
Chinese wisteria
(*Wisteria sinensis*)
Vegetables, herbs, cutting flowers as available

HOUSTON, TEXAS
RELAXATION AND ENTERTAINING
by Richard Dawson, Dawson-Estes, Inc., Houston, Texas

A single professional was the client Richard Dawson had in mind when he created this private, secure, and serene garden for relaxation and entertaining. The budget available for materials for the condominium's new landscape is $5,000.

Richard decided to give the front entrance a more elegant appearance by creating a fenced courtyard. Pads of brick laid in sand add the dignity of brick without incurring the cost of pouring slabs and mortaring masonry in place. Rectilinear beds of ground cover, annuals, and shrubs surround the pads with color and texture.

Within the courtyard, the trickle of a fountain adds ambience and a refreshing quality to the space. A crape myrtle shades the small, intimate area and provides a sense of vertical scale beside the two-story structure. Vines climb a diamond-patterned support along a wall, quickly adding the geometric formality of an espalier. A wall-mounted planter makes it easy to repeat the bright flowers that flourish at the foot of the fountain, bringing color to eye level.

Along the north side yard, a storage area for garbage, recycling, and firewood is conveniently located beside a gravel walkway. The path leads into the backyard past a vegetable, flower, and herb garden.

Brick-on-sand pads are repeated outside the living room, lending the overall design an effective cohesion. The pads lead to a patio sheltered by clusters of tree-form ligustrums. These limbed-up shrubs will not outgrow the space and rarely require pruning. Azaleas and pittosporums add colorful accents and evergreen foliage for year-round appeal. A curved seat wall is the perfect touch for a pleasant retreat and gathering spot.

Centering the backyard design, a rectangular panel of lawn makes grass a formal element in the composition. A pair of swings faces the lawn, suspended from a wisteria-covered arbor, creating a charming destination that doubles as a focal point.

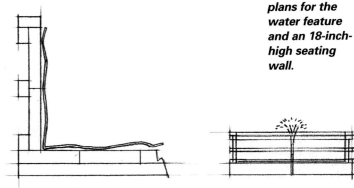

Construction details show plans for the water feature and an 18-inch-high seating wall.

Outdoor living space is maximized in this design. An exercise pool becomes the focal point of the landscape. The attractive, sheltered courtyard in front reclaims an area for private use that is usually overlooked by homeowners because of its potentially high visibility.

Buddleja

Privacy side gate

Decomposed granite

Vines on wood trellis

Perennials, grasses and seasonal color shrubs

Storage for bicycles, pool and garden equipment

Spillway into pool

Seating wall around planter and pool

Rolling gate with iron fence around frontyard

Colored, acid-washed concrete

Exercise pool

Meadow, riparian and water plants

Pond (see detail page 61)

Wood decking

Wood seating bench

Wood deck with hole for upright kayak

Buddleia   Spice bush

Fireplace (see detail page 61)

Maple with geranium underplanting

Trees
Trident maple
    (Acer buergerianum)
Mayten tree
    (Maytenus boaria)
Fruitless olive
    (Olea europaea 'Swan Hill')

Shrubs
Butterfly bush
    (Buddleja davidii)
Purple smoke tree
    (Cotinus coggygria 'Royal Purple')

Grasses & Ground Covers
Cranesbill
    (Geranium × cantabrigiense
    'Biokovo')
Hardy geranium
    (G. macrorrhizum)
Japanese blood grass
    (Imperata cylindrica 'Red Baron')
Deer grass
    (Muhlenbergia rigens)
Autumn moor grass
    (Sesleria autumnalis)

Drooping sedge
    (Carex pendula)
California gray rush
    (Juncus patens)
Water milfoil
    (Myriophyllum verticillatum)
Amphibious bisort
    (Polygonum amphibium)

Water Plants
Pickerel weed
    (Pontederia cordata)
Zebra rush
    (Schoenoplectus
    tabernaemontanus 'Zebrinus')

Beds & Borders
Common yarrow
    (Achillea millefolium)
Lady's mantle
    (Alchemilla mollis)
Dutchman's pipe
    (Aristolochia californica)
Evergreen clematis
    (Clematis armandii)
Siberian iris
    (Iris sibirica)
Mexican lobelia
    (Lobelia laxiflora)

Bee balm
    (Monarda didyma)
Mexican evening primrose,
    (Oenothera berlandieri)
Beard tongue
    (Penstemon spp.)
Mexican bush sage
    (Salvia leucantha)
Verbena
    (Verbena bonariensis)
Grape
    (Vitis vinifera)

SACRAMENTO, CALIFORNIA
NATURE AND FUN

by Michael Heacox,
Michael Glassman & Associates,
Sacramento, California

Michael Heacox designed this cozy landscape for a sports-minded bachelor with a frisbee-chasing dog. Amenities make the outdoor areas work for him, including additional storage space, a run for the dog, and an interesting collection of easy-care plants that attract butterflies and birds. The backyard needed a touch of romance, as well. After installation of a lap pool, a budget of $5,000 remained to be spent.

"Our mission is to design the kind of landscape that best fits with the client's lifestyle," Michael states. "We chose a riparian theme with wood, colored concrete, and plantings that evoke a riverside environment similar to what the client would enjoy on kayaking expeditions."

Michael designed a curbside rolling gate for vehicles with a pedestrian entry door. A redwood deck sited along the front fence line features a slot cut into it for storing a kayak upright. A small pool surrounded by ornamental grasses serves as the focal point of the entry area. Concrete, colored by adding an integral mix before it is poured, forms a new front patio and walk. A rock-salt finish gives the paving an aged, textured look. Plantings for the front garden resemble a small, natural meadow to attract butterflies.

In the back garden, the tinted and textured paving is repeated to form a patio along one side of the lap pool. A redwood deck set flush with the pool coping offers a surprising amount of entertainment and sitting space. For cozy evenings outdoors, a fireplace economically constructed of concrete block and firebrick is plastered and tinted to blend in with the colors of the landscape.

Pussywillow, ornamental grasses, and other riparian woodland species surround the hardscape with the beauty of nature and require the bare minimum of maintenance. A rustic shed adds storage without intruding on the scene. The narrow side yard is ideal for a dog run paved with decomposed gravel that connects front to back for exterior access.

The exercise pool (above) includes raised bed planters integrated into the pool side walls.

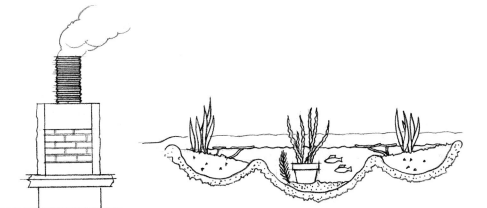

The outdoor fireplace (far left) is made of plastered concrete block and finished with granite; the front garden pond (near left) includes several depths for varied plantings and will be filled with aquatic life.

This landscape plan offers ample opportunities for dedicated gardeners. Privacy is enhanced by such techniques as the espaliered dwarf fruit tree (detail, below).

N

Bluestone pavers

Shade-loving perennials

Double-rail fence with espaliered fruit trees (see detail below)

Herb bed

Entry gate (see detail page 63)

Four vegetable beds

Sundial
Berry plantings
Windowbox with seasonal color
Rose garden

Wall trellis with vine and ground cover (see detail page 63)

Wood entry step

Barrier hedge

Brick courtyard terrace

Japanese stewartia
Vegetable teepees (see detail above)

Windowbox with seasonal color

Bench

Crabapple underplanted with vinca

Wood storage shed

Screening shrubs
6' board fence
Compost bin

Double-rail fence with espaliered fruit tree

Trees
Dwarf apples
Dwarf pears
Dwarf hardy peaches
Crabapple
　　(*Malus* 'Sugar Tyme')
Japanese stewartia
　　(*Stewartia pseudocamellia*)

Shrubs
Shrub rose
　　(*Rosa* 'White Meidiland')
Cutleaf spirea
　　(*Spiraea bumalda* 'Dolchica')
Lilac
　　(*Syringa patula* 'Miss Kim')

Barrier & Screening
Holly
　　(*Ilex × meserveae* 'China Boy' and 'China Girl')
Smooth hydrangea
　　(*Hydrangea arborescens* 'Annabelle')
Variegated privet
　　(*Ligustrum × ibolium* 'Variegata')

Grasses & Ground Covers
European wild ginger
　　(*Asarum europaeum*)
Alpine barrenwort
　　(*Epimedium alpinum*)
Periwinkle
　　(*Vinca minor*)

Beds & Borders
Astilbe
　　(*Astilbe* spp.)
Japanese painted fern
　　(*Athyrium nipponicum* 'Pictum')
Bergenia
　　(*Bergenia cordifolia*)
Erect thornless blackberry
　　(*Rubus* 'Navajo')
Clematis
　　(*Clematis* 'Etoile Violette')
Fringed bleeding heart
　　(*Dicentra eximia* 'Alba')

Bishop's hat
　　(*Epimedium grandiflorum*)
Daylily
　　(*Hemerocallis* 'Happy Returns')
Plantain lily
　　(*Hosta* hybrid)
Disease resistant raspberry
　　(*Raspberry* 'Jewel')
Strawberry
　　(*Strawberry* 'Allstair' and 'Honeoye')

WHITINSVILLE, MASSACHUSETTS
CONVENIENCE AND GARDENING
by Barbara Gaudette, Landscape Designer, Whitinsville, Massachusetts

The end-unit condominium is a better investment than renting an apartment for a couple in their twenties with a toddler. Barbara Gaudette created a basic landscape for a young family that includes some privacy and a safe area for playing.

"We had to work within a small budget—$5,000 over two years—so this plan allows for the clients to do most of the labor of brick-laying and planting," Barbara explains.

She designed a serene entry courtyard with access controlled by a lockable gate at the driveway. A brick walk and terrace enhance the image of an elegant space. Spring-blooming crabapples are the right-size tree for the small space, with roots that won't damage paving or planting. An entry trellis constructed of ½-inch copper tubing is an inexpensive addition, aging to a handsome patina with age. Clematis planted to cover the trellis add charm to the entry.

Taking advantage of the northern exposure, Barbara designed a cool, inviting shade garden flanking a bluestone walk in the side yard, making every inch of the lot count.

The couple love to garden, so Barbara included a compact vegetable garden, making it possible to harvest fresh produce from a small space. A 6-foot-high perimeter fence gives the family area privacy. An orchard of espaliered fruit trees yields fruit and adds interest to the inside view of the fence.

A lawn area within the fence provides a safe place to play within sight of adult supervision. Flowering shrubs border the lawn with easy color, leaving plenty of open space for an active child. A cedar bench in a shady nook provides adults with a place to sit and enjoy the view of the garden.

Barbara planned an inconspicuous corner for the couple to build their own storage shed. The backyard is enclosed on two sides by a wooden two-rail fence with wire fencing attached to it.

"My approach was to design a landscape that could change with the changing needs of the family," Barbara explains. "For example, there are no poured slabs in places like the children's play area that would be difficult to remove once the children are grown if the owners then wish to convert the space to other uses."

The vegetable garden is viewed through a decorative gate (above, and construction detail below right). A trellis of copper tubing (below left) and the handsome gate with copper tubing inserts can be constructed of redwood, cedar, or less-costly pressure-treated material.

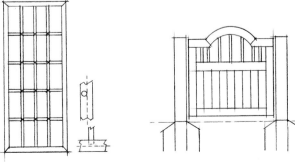

Because of close neighbors and the street, privacy
and safety solutions are important objectives for
each of these four designs. A side elevation (page 65)
shows how this site slopes to a public walk in front.

SITE SIX:
OLDER HOME
IN CENTRAL CITY

Nearly every city in America has a neighborhood of turn-of-the-century homes similar to this one.

Though such neighborhoods were always considered "in town," their cities have grown, giving areas an urban flavor. The location, close to downtown offices and shopping, is convenient. Public sidewalks, mature shade trees, and architectural charm are area assets. Safety concerns, traffic noise, lack of privacy, and small lots are typical challenges to living in these neighborhoods.

This house is a two-story structure containing about 3,500 square feet of living space. A detached garage set in the back of the lot is accessible by a long drive. A straight and narrow walkway extends from the public sidewalk to the stoop entry at the front porch. Small front yards like this one often slope sharply from the porch down to the sidewalk.

Modernizing the landscape must achieve privacy and security, maximize the usefulness of large spaces, and diffuse the impact of traffic passing by the property. Old and deteriorated plants need to be renovated or replaced by attractive and functional plantings.

The handsome finished landscape incorporates solutions for safety, privacy, curb appeal, and outdoor recreation with layers of plantings and new walks and patios.

Beds & Borders

Five-fingered fern
(*Adiantum aleuticum*)
New York aster
(*Aster novi-belgii*)
Winter-blooming bergenia
(*Bergenia crassifolia*)
Snow-in-summer
(*Cerastium tomentosum*)

Common bleeding heart
(*Dicentra spectabilis*)
Lenten rose
(*Helleborus orientalis*)
Plantain lily
(*Hosta spp.*)
Lavender
(*Lavandula spp.*)

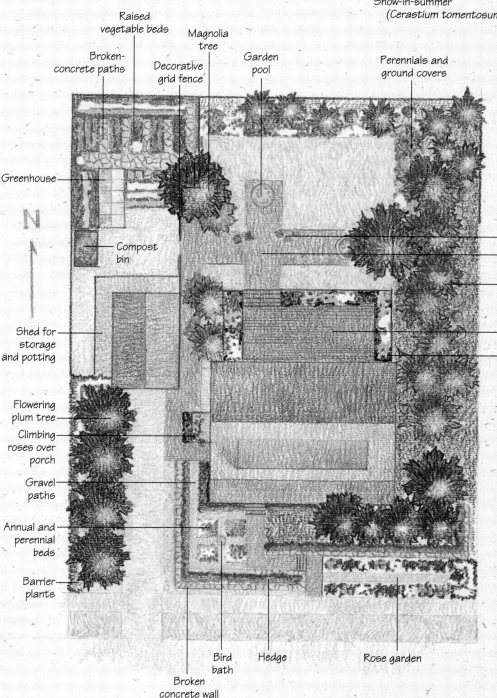

Raised vegetable beds
Broken-concrete paths
Magnolia tree
Decorative grid fence
Garden pool
Perennials and ground covers
Greenhouse
Compost bin
Pots of color
Bricks on sand base
Amelanchier trees under-planted with shrubs, shade perennials & ground covers
Bleached-wood deck
Raised bed planter (see detail page 67)
Shed for storage and potting
Flowering plum tree
Climbing roses over porch
Gravel paths
Annual and perennial beds
Barrier plants
Bird bath
Hedge
Rose garden
Broken concrete wall

Trees

Serviceberry
(*Amelanchier canadensis*)
Saucer magnolia
(*Magnolia × soulangiana*)
Chinese pistache
(*Pistacia chinensis*)
Flowering plum
(*Prunus cerasifera* 'Atropurpurea')
Scarlet oak
(*Quercus coccinea*)

Barrier & Screening

Colorado blue spruce
(*Picea pungens glauca*)
Firethorn
(*Pyracantha* 'Watereri')
American arborvitae
(*Thuja occidentalis*)

Shrubs

Flowering maple
(*Abutilon vitifolium*)
Dwarf boxwood
(*Buxus sempervirens*)
Scotch heather
(*Calluna vulgaris*)
Japanese camellia
(*Camellia japonica*)

Flowering quince
(*Chaenomeles spp.*)
Deutzia
(*Deutzia elegantissima*)
Big-leaf hydrangea
(*Hydrangea macrophylla*)
Oakleaf hydrangea
(*H. quercifolia*)

Chinese pieris
(*Pieris forrestii*)
Lady Banks' rose
(*Rosa banksiae*)
Hybrid tea
(*Rosa spp.*)
Cherokee rose
(*R. laevigata*)

Grasses & Ground Covers

Carpet bugle
(*Ajuga reptans*)
English ivy
(*Hedera helix* 'Needlepoint')
Creeping mahonia
(*Mahonia repens*)

SEATTLE, WASHINGTON
BEAUTY AND CONVENIENCE

by Robert Chittock, Robert Chittock & Associates, Seattle, Washington

Robert Chittock had a $10,000 budget to refresh this landscape and make the small, urban lot more livable. His design is for a single, middle-aged professional who is an empty-nester. Giving the home and property a more elegant entry was a priority. Adding a retreat in the back and ensuring nice views from within the house looking out into the yard were other goals.

Robert began his design at the public walk. A row of roses added to one side of the front yard balances beds of seasonal color surrounding a birdbath on the opposite side. Together, these plantings will provide a fresh, colorful look right away. Low walls, built inexpensively from broken concrete, help define the front yard spaces. Hedges of trimmed boxwood and arborvitae do the same, forming tidy borders that stay green all year.

Robert's design replaces the narrow entry walk with a broad walkway and series of steps, angled for added interest. Paving is brick laid on sand, which costs less than brick mortared to a slab; irregularities that will occur as bricks shift slightly match the look of the older house. The same technique was used to create a new walkway that connects the driveway to the backyard.

A dense grid fence line along the garage separates it from the rear living spaces. In the northwest corner, a vegetable garden has been established adjacent to a greenhouse and composting area. A shed roof added around the garage provides a protective overhang sheltering a potting bench area that also provides storage space.

Dining room doors open onto a new bleached wood deck, making this outdoor spot ideal for fresh air meals and entertaining. A brick patio provides a second outdoor retreat for relaxing or gathering with friends. Two small water features contribute the pleasant sound of moving water, a trick which helps mask intrusive noises common to city living. A lawn area in the northeast quadrant of the property, small enough to mow quickly, helps create an illusion of spaciousness by contrasting with layers of plantings that surround it.

A new entry (above) features retaining walls of recycled concrete paving and beds of roses and seasonal color. A planter box adds interest to the new deck (left).

The new terrace entry and rear patio welcome those who enter the house; the pergola ties the garage and kitchen to the kitchen garden.

Shrubs

Japanese boxwood
   (*Buxus microphylla* 'Winter Gem')
Carolina allspice
   (*Calycanthus floridus*)
Gilt-edge elaeagnus
   (*Elaeagnus × ebbengei* 'Gilt Edge')
Redvein enkianthus
   (*Enkianthus campanulatus*)
Blue holly
   (*Ilex × meserveae* 'Blue Boy')

Chinese juniper
   (*Juniperus chinensis* 'Blue Point')
Pfitzer juniper
   (*J. × media* 'Pfitzeriana')
Wax myrtle
   (*Myrica cerifera*)
Dwarf heavenly bamboo
   (*Nandina domestica* 'Nana')
Carolina cherry laurel
   (*Prunus caroliniana*)

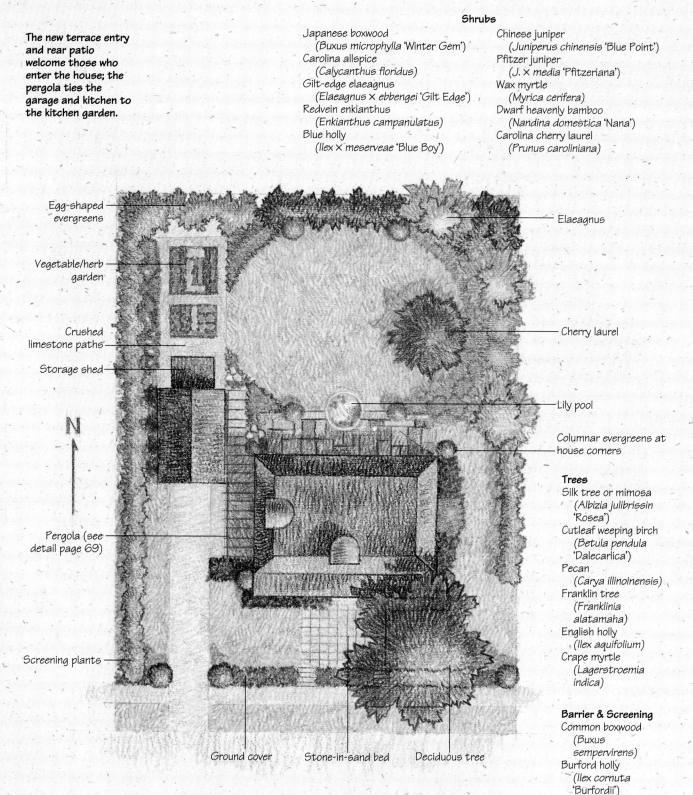

Egg-shaped evergreens

Vegetable/herb garden

Crushed limestone paths

Storage shed

N

Pergola (see detail page 69)

Screening plants

Elaeagnus

Cherry laurel

Lily pool

Columnar evergreens at house corners

Trees
Silk tree or mimosa
   (*Albizia julibrissin* 'Rosea')
Cutleaf weeping birch
   (*Betula pendula* 'Dalecarlica')
Pecan
   (*Carya illinoinensis*)
Franklin tree
   (*Franklinia alatamaha*)
English holly
   (*Ilex aquifolium*)
Crape myrtle
   (*Lagerstroemia indica*)

Ground cover   Stone-in-sand bed   Deciduous tree

Barrier & Screening
Common boxwood
   (*Buxus sempervirens*)
Burford holly
   (*Ilex cornuta* 'Burfordii')
Hybrid holly
   (*Ilex* 'Nellie R. Stevens')
Yew pine
   (*Podocarpus macrophyllus*)
Japanese yew
   (*Taxus cuspidata*)

Beds & Borders
Bear's breech
   (*Acanthus mollis*)
Goat's beard
   (*Aruncus aethusifolius*)
Black snakeroot
   (*Cimicifuga racemosa*)
Corydalis cheilanthifolia

Grasses & Ground Covers
Dwarf plumbago
   (*Ceratostigma plumbaginoides*)
Rockspray cotoneaster
   (*Cotoneaster microphyllus*)
Mondo grass
   (*Ophiopogon japonicus*)
Asiatic jasmine
   (*Trachelospermum asiaticum*)

JACKSON, MISSISSIPPI
RELAXATION AND ENTERTAINING
by Overton Moore, Landscape Architect, Jackson, Mississippi

The pond off the patio and pergola are new focal points (left); an architectural detail of the pergola framing (below) shows design and construction technique.

Primary goals of this design, formulated for a couple in their late twenties, included attaining privacy and adding areas suitable for small-scale entertaining. Their budget for materials was $15,000. To stretch their funds, the plan includes plantings and construction projects that can be tackled as do-it-yourself undertakings.

Overton Moore employed a sequential design strategy. Spaces and plantings adjacent to the house are formal in design, while looser, curvilinear lines transition into informal spaces as the landscape progresses away from the architecture.

Overton replaced the narrow entry walk with a broad terrace to create a welcoming entry court. All front yard plantings were replaced with new foundation shrubs and beds. Conifers anchor the corners of the house with classic style, contrasting with low ground covers. A formal pergola now links the garage to the kitchen entry.

Most of the rear yard is devoted to an elliptical swath of lawn beside a new rear terrace. Together, the lawn and paving provide ample room for entertaining. A lily pool situated along the far edge of the terrace commands a view of the entire garden, directing views inward and away from neighboring properties. Evergreen hedges incorporated into existing plantings add privacy.

This innovative design provides wheelchair access throughout, from the front entry to all parts of the rear gardens.

Trees
Chinese hibiscus
(pruned as tree)
(Hibiscus rosa-sinensis)
Crape myrtle
(Lagerstroemia indica)
Wax myrtle
(Myrica cerifera)
Sweet olive
(Osmanthus fragrans)

Lily-of-the-Nile
(Agapanthus africanus)
Cast-iron plant
(Aspidistra elatior)
Holly Fern
(Cyrtomium falcatum)
Daylily
(Hemerocallis spp.)
Lily turf
(Liriope muscari 'Evergreen Giant')

Beds & Borders
Pink allamanda
(Mandevilla splendens)
Walking iris
(Neomarica gracilis)
Boston fern
(Nephrolepsis exaltata 'Bostoniensis')
Vegetables, herbs and collectable plants as desired

Brick ramp (see illustration page 71

Trellised and benched area for orchids and bonsai

Seating bench

Brick-in-sand terrace and paths

Wood deck

Flowering shrubs

Water feature in raised bed (see detail page 71)

Greenhouse

Hydrangeas

Work tables

Ferns and perennials

6' high fence

Shrubs
Japanese boxwood
(Buxus microphylla japonica)
Azalea
(Rhododendron 'Snow', 'Duc de Rohan', 'Southern Charm')
Sandankwa viburnum
(Viburnum suspensum)

Potting bench

Grill

Plant bench

Trellis with vines and bench for sun-sensitive plant collection

Grasses & Ground Covers
Creeping fig
(Ficus pumila)
Shore juniper
(Juniperus conferta)
Mondo grass
(Ophiopogon japonicus)
Goldmoss sedum
(Sedum acre)
Asiatic jasmine
(Trachelospermum asiaticum

4' wide gate

Crape myrtles

N

Screening plants

Brick planter walk

Brick-in-sand ramp

Oak underplanted with ground covers

Barrier & Screening
Carolina jessamine
(Gelsemium sempervirens)
Bigleaf hydrangea
(Hydrangea macrophylla)
Japanese privet
(Ligustrum japonicum)
Confederate jasmine
(Trachelospermum jasminoides)

JACKSONVILLE, FLORIDA
NATURE AND GARDENING
by Robert Hartwig, Hartwig & Associates, Jacksonville, Florida

This design is for a fortyish couple. In addition to addressing the problems of an urban lot, it includes barrier-free access throughout the site and space for gardening from a wheelchair. The budget for materials is $15,000, not including the greenhouse, to be purchased as a kit.

Robert Hartwig designed a new landscape that is both pretty and accessible. Grading the front yard to form a gentle incline made it possible to remove the steps to the porch and replace them with a ramp. Brick-on-sand walks provide access to beds on both sides of the walk. The extra-wide, pleasantly inviting walkways accomodate a wheelchair.

The backyard is equally appealing and handicap-friendly. A ramp leads from the kitchen and dining area to a series of level hard surfaces, including a cookout area sheltered by an arbor. A potting area and storage cabinet outside the greenhouse were designed at a height comfortable for the physically challenged gardener. Benches beneath an arbor on the south side of the lot quickly became a favorite place for puttering with potted plants.

Raised beds contain a kaleidoscope of colorful plants that thrive in the clients' frost-free climate. Hydrangea, lily-of-the-Nile, and hibiscus fill beds within reach. Confederate jasmine and mandevilla grow over the edge of planters and tumble downward. Plantings are concentrated along the perimeter of the property to add privacy and block unwanted views of adjacent areas. A modest water feature, tucked into a glen in the southeast corner of the lot, is positioned to be admired from the backyard walkway.

Planter beds at wheelchair height and hard-surface ramps and walks make gardening easily accessible. (above).

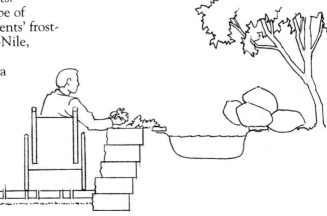

Both beds and garden features, such as this pond, are elevated for easy access and viewing (left).

The new design incorporates numerous recreational amenities for an active family.

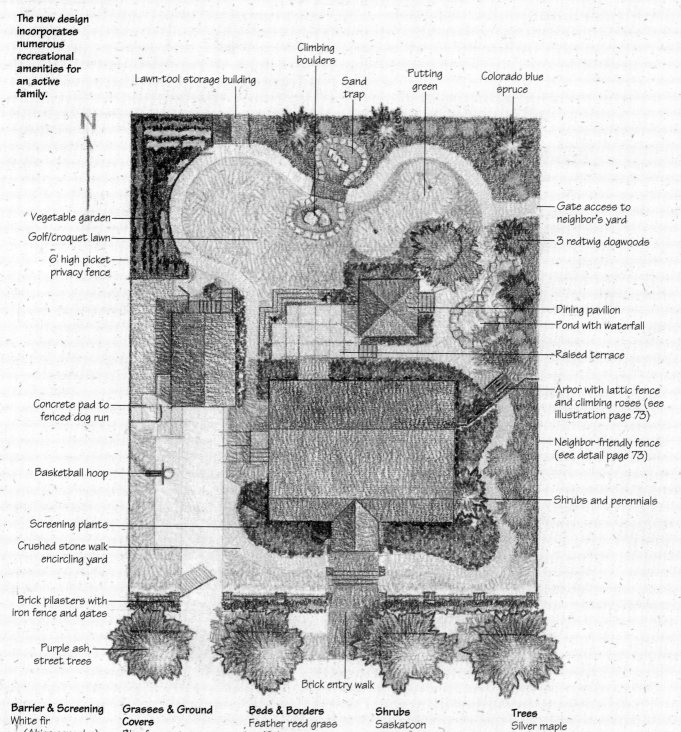

Lawn-tool storage building

Climbing boulders

Sand trap

Putting green

Colorado blue spruce

N

Vegetable garden

Golf/croquet lawn

6' high picket privacy fence

Gate access to neighbor's yard

3 redtwig dogwoods

Dining pavilion

Pond with waterfall

Raised terrace

Concrete pad to fenced dog run

Arbor with lattic fence and climbing roses (see illustration page 73)

Neighbor-friendly fence (see detail page 73)

Basketball hoop

Shrubs and perennials

Screening plants

Crushed stone walk encircling yard

Brick pilasters with iron fence and gates

Purple ash, street trees

Brick entry walk

Barrier & Screening
White fir
 (Abies concolor)
Mockorange
 (Philadelphus
 virginalis
 'Minnesota
 Snowflake')
Colorado blue
 spruce
 (Picea pungens
 'Glauca')
Arrowwood viburnum
 (Viburnum
 dentatum)

Grasses & Ground Covers
Blue fescue
 (Festuca ovina
 "Glauca')
Sweet woodruff
 (Galium odoratum)
Improved bluegrass
 varieties and blends
Creeping juniper
 (Juniperus communis
 'Silver Miles')
Creeping mahonia
 (Mahonia repens)
Lamb's ears
 (Stachys byzantina)

Beds & Borders
Feather reed grass
 (Calamagrostis
 acutifolia 'Stricta')
Purple coneflower
 (Echinacea purpurea)
Cranesbill
 (Geranium
 sanguineum)
Daylily
 (Hemerocallis spp.)
Plantain lily
 (Hosta spp.)
Gayfeather
 (Liatris spicata
 'Kobold')

Shrubs
Saskatoon
 (Amelanchier alnifolia
 'Regent')
Redtwig dogwood
 (Cornus stolonifera)
Sweet mockorange
 (Philadelphus
 coronarius)
Current
 (Ribes odoratum)
Roses
Spirea
 (Spiraea japonica)
Chinese lilac
 (Syringa chinensis
 'Alba')

Trees
Silver maple
 (Acer saccharinum)
Russian hawthorn
 (Crataegus ambigua)
Thornless dotted hawthorn
 (Crataegus punctata
 inermis)
Purple ash
 (Fraxinus americana 'Autumn
 Purple')
Weeping higan cherry
 (Prunus serrulata 'Pendula')
Swamp white oak
 (Quercus bicolor)
Red oak
 (Quercus rubra)

DENVER, COLORADO
WELCOME AND FUN
by Richard Marshall, DHM Designs, Denver, Colorado

Richard Marshall's plan fits an astonishing number of activity areas into the small lot without making it seem crowded. Designed for a large family— a couple, their five children ranging in ages from 7 to 16, and one grandparent—the landscape balances the needs of children and adults. A welcoming front entry, plenty of amenities for children, and outdoor spots for the grownups are included in the budget of $10,000, to be spread over two years.

"With so many active children in the family, it was imperative to make an environment that would lure them outside and keep them involved and entertained," Richard comments.

To create a generous, welcoming entry, Richard used a simple approach for the front yard. A wrought iron gate hung between a pair of brick pilasters gives the entry presence. The narrow walkway was replaced with a wide brick walk leading from curbside to widened entry steps that double as sitting spots for children. Expanding the covered front porch provides outdoor family space. A paved extension of the driveway is home to a basketball hoop. Wrap-around foundation beds are filled with durable ground covers and shrubs.

A hard-surface pathway borders the beds, making it easy to keep planting areas and lawns separate and neat. The pathway winds its way around the house, providing a continuous course for wheeled toys and skates. The path passes beneath a grape arbor on the east side of the house, signaling passage into the back yard. A pond and waterfall on the right add the peaceful sight and sound of water. A new patio and raised gazebo pavilion are large enough for the whole family to dine outside, yet cozy enough to be a relaxing area for adults.

The pathway connects through a gate with a friendly neighbor's property. The curving grassed area provides open space for play and includes a putting green. Tucked in the northeast corner, a vegetable and herb garden gives family members of all ages an opportunity to plant and pick fresh harvests. Tools and toys are kept handy by a Victorian-style storage shed.

Richard made the most of space; stairs attached to the north side of the garage lead to a rooftop deck and hot tub. Heavily planted perimeters add privacy to the backyard.

Viewed through an arbor, the gazebo anchors the new rear patio (above).

Drawing (left) illustrates the technique for setting fence posts correctly.

This home occupies only a small portion of a 1-acre lot. Several mature trees remain in the backyard, but the front yard was bulldozed to provide a building pad for the new home. Challenges for designers include a need for distinctive personality for this suburban property and stronger curb appeal.

N

SITE SEVEN:
NEW SUBURBAN HOME,
LARGE VIEW LOT

The outer edges of suburbia continue to be developed, as the pattern of immigration from city to countryside continues. Homeowners get more house and land. They may have to fight traffic during their daily commute to work, but they come home to quiet residential streets and the feeling of being out in the country.

This home is a prime example of a popular housing choice. It is newly constructed, offering about 2,000 square feet in living space.

The house sits fairly close to the road on a 1-acre hillside lot. The property backs up to a scenic area offering attractive views from all rear rooms. There are several mature trees in back, but the front yard was bulldozed to provide a building pad, leaving the house looking a bit stark and isolated.

Creating an air of establishment is necessary to make the architecture seem at home on its lot.

Typical problems facing suburban homeowners include a lack of streetside privacy in the front yard as well as a lack of distinctive personality, making a weak first impression of the home.

The large house seems to dwarf the treeless front yard. Unclaimed and unused space in the backyard is the result of untamed sloping terrain.

Lush plantings of colorful trees, shrubs, and bedding plants create a garden for the homeowner and a joy for the viewer in this new landscape.

Shrubs

Japanese camellia
(*Camellia japonica*)
Big-leaf hydrangea
(*Hydrangea macrophylla*)
Drooping leucothoe
(*Leucothoe fontanesiana*)

Spicebush
(*Lindera benzoin*)
Peony
(*Paeonia spp.*)
Mugo pine
(*Pinus mugo mugo*)
Cumberland azalea
(*Rhododendron bakeri*)

Belgian Indica hybrid azalea
(*Rhododendron hybrids*)
Oconee azalea
(*Rhododendron flammeum*)
Shrub roses
(*Rosa spp.*)

N

Barrier and screening plants

Pavilion (see detail page 77)

Stone steps in grass

Boxwood hedge frames lawn

Azalea, bulb, and wildflower drifts

Stepping stones in decomposed granite create a meandering path through shade gardens.

Fence and gate to side garden

Deciduous trees ring property

Flowering shrubs and perennials

Paved path from garage to golf course

Compost, potting and storage area

Rose-covered kitchen garden fence

Garden bench

Raised vegetable and herb beds

Barrier and screening plants

Large, step-down brick terrace

Colorful perennials and flowering shrubs along driveway (see detail this page)

Flowering shrubs and perennials

Trees

Japanese maple
(*Acer palmatum* 'Burgundy Lace')
Red maple
(*A. rubrum*)
American sweet gum
(*Liquidambar styraciflua*)
Tulip tree
(*Liriodendron tulipifera*)
Southern magnolia
(*Magnolia grandiflora*)
Weeping willow-leafed pear
(*Pyrus salicifolia* 'Pendula')
Swamp white oak
(*Quercus bicolor*)
Mountain stewartia
(*Stewartia ovata*)

Barrier & Screening

Common boxwood
(*Buxus sempervirens*)
Mountain laurel
(*Kalmia latifolia*)
Leatherleaf viburnum
(*Viburnum rhytidophyllum*)

Beds & Borders

Astilbe
(*Astilbe arendsii*)
Blackberry lily
(*Belamcanda chinensis*)
Butterfly bush
(*Buddleja davidii*)
Bellflower
(*Campanula spp.*)
Crinum
(*Crinum × powellii* 'Album')

Iris
(*Iris spp.*)
Ligularia
(*Ligularia dentata*)
Bee balm
(*Monarda didyma*)
Summer phlox
(*Phlox paniculata*)
Climbing rose
(*Rosa* 'Climbing Iceberg')

ATLANTA, GEORGIA
BEAUTY AND GARDENING
by Mary Palmer Dargan, Landscape Architect, Hugh Dargan & Associates, Atlanta, Georgia

Mary Palmer Dargan designed this plan for a single man in his fifties who wants privacy for outdoor settings but who wishes to retain views of the golf course behind his lot. A substantial garden for flowers, vegetables, and herbs, an outdoor pavilion and other entertainment areas, and golf cart access from this property to the course are included. The landscape budget is $10,000 a year for the next three years.

Mary Palmer placed a garden for edible and ornamental harvests in a previously overlooked sunny place beside the driveway. Because it is in the front yard, she took care to make the garden attractive and to screen it from direct view with a handsome fence covered with climbing roses. A gate at one end leads to a compost and potting area with storage bins for amendments and garden tools.

Behind the house, the existing rear patio was enlarged to provide ample room for entertaining. The patio looks out onto a grand view of the golf course, across a lawn terraced to tame the precipitous terrain. Curved stone borders highlight the undulating shape of grassed areas. The lawn narrows as it recedes, terminating at a garden pavilion that serves as the focal point of the long sightline. The pavilion frames the view to the course itself and houses a hammock and lounges, making it a destination.

White oak, tulip poplar, red maple, and sweet gum mix with existing plantings and add welcome shade in summer and dazzling color in fall. Shrubs placed around the perimeter enhance privacy. Other amenities include a grassy private garden accented with sculpture, a shade garden with wildflowers and shade-tolerant perennials, and paths that wind through the property for nature hiking. Golf cart access is provided by a path connecting the golf course to the garage—through new doors installed in the back wall.

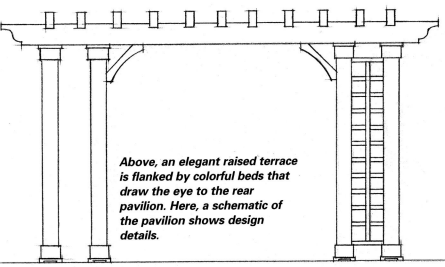

Above, an elegant raised terrace is flanked by colorful beds that draw the eye to the rear pavilion. Here, a schematic of the pavilion shows design details.

This interesting landscape uses detail to create a nature lover's garden with places to stop and enjoy the views woven into the fabric of the design.

Little bluestem
(Schizachyrium scoparius)
Windflower
(Anemone blanda)
Butterfly weed
(Asclepias tuberosa)
Asparagus fern
(Asparagus setaceus)
Basket-of-gold
(Aurinia saxatilis)
Sideoats grama
(Bouteloua curtipendula)
Indian paintbrush
(Castilleja coccinea)
Chamomile
(Chamaemelum nobile)
Ice plant
(Delospermum nubigerum)

Beds & Borders

Dwarf pinks
(Dianthus 'Tiny Rubies')
Purple coneflower
(Echinacea purpurea)
Sulphur buckwheat
(Eriogonum umbellatum)
Bronze fennel
(Foeniculum vulgare)
Daylilies
(Hemerocallis spp.)
Perky Sue
(Hymenoxys grandiflora)
Miniature iris
(Iris spp.)
Prairie flax
(Linum perenne lewisii)
Blackfoot daisy
(Melampodium leucanthum)

Miniature daffodils
(Narcissus spp.)
Oregano
(Origanum vulgare)
Scarlet bugler
(Penstemon barbatus)
Russian sage
(Perovskia 'Blue Spire')
Mexican hat
(Ratibida columnifera)
Black-eyed Susan
(Rudbeckia fulgida)
Common sage
(Salvia officinalis)
Blue sage
(S. superba 'Blue Hills')
Stonecrop
(Sedum spurium 'Dragon's Blood')

Barrier & Screening

Curl-leaf mountain mahogany
(Cercocarpus ledifolius)
Juniper
(Juniperus virginiana 'Idylwild')
Piñon pine
(Pinus edulis)
Korean pine
(Pinus koraiensis)
Silver buffalo berry
(Shepherdia argentea)

Two benches
Hammock
Native perennials, bulbs and grasses
Locust and walnut trees
Swales to keep water run-off on-site

Trails of bark mulch or crushed stone

Retaining wall with gate (see detail page 79)

Flagstone patio

Buffalo grass lawn

Deciduous native trees

Barrier and screening plants

Perennials and flowering shrubs

Flagstone entry walk

Gravel driveway

Fruit orchard
Cedar grape arbor
Fenced vegetable garden
Kitchen herb garden

N

Trees
Apple
Apricot
Western redbud
(Cercis occidentalis)
Cherry
Honeylocust
(Gleditsia triacanthos)
Black walnut
(Juglans nigra)
Peach
Plum
Quaking aspen
(Populus tremuloides)
Amur chokecherry
(Prunus maackii)

Shrubs

Mountain mahogany
(Cercocarpus montanus)
Rubber rabbitbrush
(Chrysothamnus nauseosus)
Cliff rose
(Cowania mexicana stansburiana)
Apache plume
(Fallugia paradoxa)
Fendler's cliffbush
(Fendlera rupicola)

Gooseberry
(Ribes 'Pixwell')
English lavender
(Lavandula angustifolia 'Munstead')
Lavender
(L. × intermedia 'Provence')
Raspberry
(Ribes 'Heritage' and 'Canby')
Squawbush
(Rhus trilobata)

Golden currant
(Ribes aureum)
Rugosa rose
(Rosa rugosa ramanas 'Will Alderman')
Rosemary
(Rosemarinus officinalis 'Huntington Blue' and 'Majorca Pink')
Blue elderberry
(Sambucus mexicana)

Grasses & Ground Covers
Buffalograss
(Buchloe dactyloides)
Blue gammagrass
(Bouteloua gracilis)
Snow-in-summer
(Cerastium tomentosum)
Woodland strawberry
(Fragaria vesca)
Creeping mahonia
(Mahonia repens)

SANTA FE, NEW MEXICO
RELAXATION AND NATURE
by Ben Haggard, Regenesis, Santa Fe, New Mexico

Ben Haggard designed this plan for a young couple with two school-age children who would learn about nature from this landscape, while including intimate spaces for relaxation. The budget for materials was $14,000.

First, Ben eliminated the white concrete driveway that dominated the front yard. He designed a replacement drive with a gravel surface typical of the Albuquerque area, which reflects less heat and glare than paving. The new driveway follows a different path, curving to the garage and providing extra parking and turn-around space without passing in front of the house. This eliminates the sight of vehicles from the first view of the home. A new entry patio of flagstone replaces the small original slab, giving the exterior area interesting texture and color. The larger patio size relates to the scale of the house, making the entry more comfortable.

Outside the kitchen, a small herb garden takes advantage of the sunny exposure. A large production garden is located near the garage. Just beyond, a grape arbor and orchard of mixed fruit trees makes gardening a rewarding pastime.

Groves of Arizona black walnut and black locusts interplanted with existing Rio Grande cottonwoods serve as a windbreak surrounding the property and provide shade. A system of paths and switchbacks snake through the property, leading invitingly away from the house. A hammock and benches strategically placed off the trails make stopping to enjoy the scenery of this mini nature preserve a pleasant option. All of the plantings added to enhance the site were chosen for drought tolerance, including many native species. This design approach is appropriate in an arid region where rainfall is scarce and water is a precious commodity.

Varied species create a garden palette that can be enjoyed from the new system of paths on the property (above). Retaining walls add interest by varying levels within the garden (below).

The redesigned entry and front beds enhance the curb appeal and present a welcoming invitation to visitors in this new landscape.

Barrier & Screening
Strawberry tree
(Arbutus unedo 'Oktoberfest')
Ceanothus
(Ceanothus 'Coast Whitethorn')
Pacific wax myrtle
(Myrica californica)
California laurel
(Umbellularia californica)

Grasses & Ground Covers
Point Reyes creeper
(Ceanothus gloriosus)
Creeping St. John's wort
(Hypericum calycinum)
Blue star creeper
(Laurentia fluviatilis)
Japanese spurge
(Pachysandra terminalis)

Apple 'Gravenstein',
Jonathon', 'Northern Spy'
Kousa dogwood
(Cornus kousa 'Rosabella')
Carriere hawthorn
(Crataegus × lavallei)
Japanese red pine
(Pinus densiflora)

Trees
Scotch pine
(Pinus sylvestris)
Japanese black pine
(Pinus thunbergii)
Flowering cherry
(Prunus serrulata 'Pink Star')
Scarlet oak
(Quercus coccinea)
Pin oak
(Quercus palustris)

Beds & Borders
Western bleeding heart
(Dicentra formosa)
Common foxglove
(Digitalis purpurea)
Cranesbill
(Geranium sanguineum
Plantain lily
(Hosta hybrids)
Japanese iris
(I. ensata)
Yellow Siberian iris
(I. forrestii)
Fountain grass
(Pennisetum alopecuroides)

Terraced raised bed garden with dwarf shrubs and sun perennials (see detail above)

Outdoor kitchen

Trellis structure over patio

Apple tree

Deciduous trees underplanted with native bulbs, ferns, and perennials

Evergreen tree underplanted with ferns and shade perennials

Shade perennials and ferns

Grapes and kiwi vines trellised on side of garage

Raised vegetable/herb beds

Barrier and screening plants

Flowering shrubs, bulbs, and summer color

Gravel path (see detail page 81)

Trellised fence with climbing roses, azaleas and bulbs in front

Blueberries

Pergola entrance to vegetable garden

N

Shrubs

English boxwood
(Buxus sempervirens
Winter daphne
(Daphne odora)
Enkianthus
(Enkianthus perulatus)

Hollywood juniper
(Juniperus chinensis 'Kaizuka')
Japanese garden juniper
(J. c. procumbens)

Drooping leucothoe
(Leucothoe fontanesiana)
Lily-of-the-valley shrub
(Pieris japonica)
Satsuki hybrid azaleas
(Rhododendron 'Satsuki')

Climbing rose
(Rosa 'Sunset')
David viburnum
(Viburnum davidii)
Doublefile viburnum
(V. plicatum tomemtosum)

PORTLAND, OREGON
WELCOME AND ENTERTAINING
by John Herbst, Jr., Landscape Architect, John Herbst, Jr. & Associates, Portland, Oregon

When the same large house and lot are located within a resort area, the house is an ideal choice for a vacation home today and a primary residence in the future. John Herbst, Jr. designed this landscape for a professional couple who entertain often. They have no children of their own, but many nieces and nephews are frequent visitors. The budget of $40,000 for materials is to be spent over three years. The plan is low-maintenance in the off-season, when the owners will initially be away from the property.

John began by redesigning the front entry to make it more gracious and appealing. He added three trellises along the front property line and trained roses on them for a touch of color at streetside. Next, he enlarged the front walk and flanked it with foundation beds filled with spring and summer color. Viburnums anchor the front planting scheme.

The sunny southern side yard becomes a garden spot, devoted to herbs, berries, and vegetables growing in raised beds. Grape and kiwi vines twine their way up a trellis mounted on the garage wall. On the west side of the structure, a new patio houses an outdoor kitchen and picnic table under a pergola cover, perfect for entertaining. A terraced perennial garden makes the most of the slope beyond the patio.

A gravel path leads from the rear patio to a shade garden retreat. Ferns, fuchsias, and hostas grow in the shelter of conifers. Perimeter plantings of shrubs and ground covers add privacy and frame the view of a lake and golf course to the rear of the site.

A view from the street repeats the welcoming theme with low fences festooned with roses and unobstructed views into the garden (above).

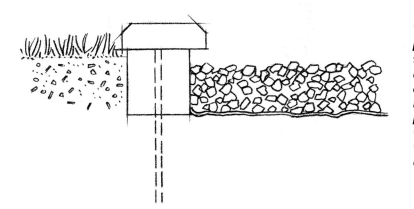

The gravel paving throughout this design offers a casual effect. It is held in place by pressure-treated wood edging with a beveled cap.

This user-friendly landscape complete with lap pool is an irresistible lure to the kids in the family. The tree house (top detail) gives them ample space to romp.

Trees

Eastern redbud
(*Cercis canadensis* 'Silver Cloud')
Alaska cedar
(*Chamaecyparis nootkatensis*)
Flowering dogwood
(*Cornus florida* 'Rubra')
Maidenhair tree
(*Ginkgo biloba* 'Saratoga')
Honeylocust
(*Gleditsia triacanthos inermis* 'Shademaster')
Weeping spruce
(*Picea pungens* 'Pendula')
Douglas fir
(*Pseudotsuga menziesii*)

Shrubs

Dwarf hinoki false cypress
(*Chamaecyparis obtusa* 'Nana Gracilis')
Holly
(*Ilex × meserveae* 'Blue Princess' and 'Blue Prince')
English cherry laurel
(*Prunus laurocerasus* 'Otto Luyken')
Rhododendron (Kurume hybrid) 'Hino-crimson'
Rhododendron
(*R.* 'Vulcan')
Japanese snowball
(*Viburnum plicatum plicatum*)

Barrier & Screening

Darwin barberry
(*Berberis darwinii*)
Variegated American holly
(*Ilex opaca* 'Stewart's Silver Crown')
Yew
(*Taxus × media* 'Roseum Elegans')
Leatherleaf viburnum
(*Viburnum × rhytidophyllum*)

Weeping evergreen

Barrier and screening plants with deciduous trees in front, underplanted with shade-loving perennials on both sides of property

Two-tiered wood retaining wall with sun-loving shrubs and flowers

Tree house

Brick pool deck and lap pool

Rock garden

Vegetable garden

Brick patio and walks (see detail page 83)

Barbeque and serving counter

Screening fence with sideyard gate

Douglas fir

Dogwoods with flowering shrubs

Yew hedge with azaleas and three honeylocust trees

Gated arbor

N

Beds & Borders

Fringed bleeding heart
(*Dicentra eximia*)
Daylily
(*Hemerocallis* hybrids)
Plantain lily
(*Hosta* 'Frances Williams')
Plantain lily
(*Hosta sieboldiana*)
Gayfeather
(*Liatris* spp.)

Purple loosestrife
(*Lythrum salicaria*)
Gloriosa daisy
(*Rudbeckia hirta*)
Sedum
(*Sedum kamtschaticum*)
Hens and chicks
(*Sempervivum tectorum*)
Lemon thyme
(*Thymus citriodorus* 'Aureus')

Grasses & Ground Covers

Carpet bugleweed
(*Ajuga reptans* 'Burgundy Glow')
Dwarf Japanese barberry
(*Berberis thunbergii* 'Crimson Pygmy')
Japanese spurge
(*Pachysandra terminalis* 'Silver Edge')

GREENLAWN, NEW YORK
CONVENIENCE AND FUN
by Raymond Rolfe, Landscape Architect, Greenlawn, New York

The large yard's potential is a selling point for a young couple with two pre-teens. Raymond Rolfe designed a family-style landscape on a budget of $16,500, not including the cost of a new lap pool, which they contracted separately.

Ray added planting beds to the front yard to enhance the initial view of the home and to add separation from the street. Corner beds and a planting area in front of the curved driveway contain dense plantings of conifers, rhododendrons, and honey locusts.

A new arbor retreat creates a destination enjoyed by the whole family or by children and adults separately. A generously proportioned brick-on-sand patio outside the family and dining rooms extends interior uses to the out-of-doors. Stairs lead down to a lap pool, where brick to match the patio and nearby walkways is repeated in the pool coping for visual unity. The fence is screened from front yard views by a stepped fence.

A perennial and vegetable garden is conveniently close to a utility shed. The attractive beds are positioned to be viewed from the pool area. Beyond the garden, a lawn extends to the farthest reaches of the property, providing a play area for the children. A tree house and rope swing tucked in the corner of the site attract children out into the landscape. A chain-link fence, finished in black to recede from view, secures the rear property line.

The pool is located in an area off the back patio, visible from the house (above).

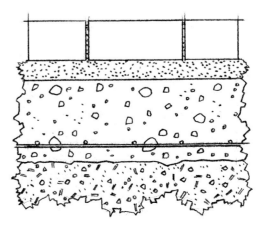

Drawing (left) illustrates technique for laying brick on sand for walks and patios.

REGIONAL PLANT LISTS

Use these lists as a quick reference to some of the more important landscape plants in your region. The plants included here have been selected for their reliability as well as their ready availability.

The illustrated profile for a tree indicates the predictable form and size it will reach after 15 to 20 years of growth. For a shrub it represents its size after four to five years of growth. Groundcovers are illustrated in their third year of growth, and perennials in their second season.

Consult the map on page 92 to locate the USDA hardiness zone for your area. Then check the zone range provided for each plant to find those likely to thrive where you live.

MIDWEST

TREES

20'
Red maple
Acer rubrum
Zones 3 to 9
12'

12'
Eastern redbud
Cercis
12' *canadensis*
Zones 3 to 9

15'
Washington
hawthorn
Crataegus
10' *phaenopyrum*
Zones 3 to 8

25'
Northern
red oak
Quercus rubra
25' Zones 4 to 8

25'
Thornless
honeylocust
Gleditsia
20' *triacanthos*
var. *inermis*
Zones 3 to 9

25'
Scotch pine
Pinus sylvestris
Zones 3 to 8
15'

SHRUBS

6'
Japanese
barberry
8' *Berberis*
thunbergii
Zones 4 to 8

8'
Inkberry
Ilex glabra
12' Zones 3 to 10

6'
Pfitzer juniper
Juniperus ×
10' *media*
'Pfitzeriana'
Zones 4 to 9

18'
Lilac
Syringa
vulgaris
15' Zones 3 to 7

3'
Japanese spirea
Spiraea japonica
4' Zones 4 to 8

10'
American
cranberrybush
viburnum
10' *Viburnum*
trilobum
Zones 4 to 8

GROUND COVERS

1'
Bergenia
Bergenia
cordifolia
1' Zones 4 to 8

1'
Bearberry
6' cotoneaster
Cotoneaster
dammeri
Zones 5 to 8

10"
Red
barrenwort
12" *Epimedium* ×
rubrum
Zones 5 to 8

3'
Wintercreeper
5' euonymus
Euonymus
fortunei
Zones 5 to 8

6"
Creeping
4' juniper
Juniperus
horizontalis
Zones 3 to 9

3'
Bush
cinquefoil
3' *Potentilla*
fruticosa
Zones 3 to 7

PERENNIALS

2'
Threadleaf
coreopsis
2' *Coreopsis*
verticillata
Zones 5 to 9

3'
Purple
coneflower
Echinacea
purpurea
2' Zones 3 to 8

2'
Daylily
Hemerocallis
2' hybrids
Zones 3 to 9

8'
Maiden grass
Miscanthus
sinensis
3' Zones 5 to 9

4'
Black-eyed
Susan
Rudbeckia
fulgida
3' Zones 3 to 8

24"
Stonecrop
Sedum
spectabile
18" Zones 3 to 9

NORTHEAST

TREES

White fir
Abies concolor
Zones 4 to 8

Japanese maple
Acer palmatum
Zones 5 to 8

Kousa
dogwood
Cornus kousa
Zones 5 to 8

European
beech
Fagus sylvatica
Zones 5 to 7

Ginkgo
Ginkgo biloba
Zones 4 to 8

Saucer
magnolia
*Magnolia ×
soulangiana*
Zones 5 to 9

Crabapple
Malus hybrids
Zones 4 to 8

Serbian spruce
Picea omorika
Zones 4 to 7

Sargent cherry
Prunus sargentii
Zones 5 to 8

Littleleaf
linden
Tilia cordata
Zones 4 to 7

SHRUBS

Summersweet
*Clethra
alnifolia*
Zones 3 to 9

Heath
Erica species
Zones 5 to 8

Large
fothergilla
*Fothergilla
major*
Zones 5 to 8

Hybrid witch
hazel
*Hamamelis ×
intermedia*
Zones 5 to 8

Common
winterberry
Ilex verticillata
Zones 4 to 8

Mountain
laurel
Kalmia latifolia
Zones 5 to 8

Japanese
andromeda
Pieris japonica
Zones 5 to 9

Evergreen
Rhododendron
Rhododendron
hybrids
Zones 5 to 8

Highbush
blueberry
*Vaccinium
corymbosum*
Zones 5 to 8

Doublefile
viburnum
*Viburnum
plicatum
tomentosum*
Zones 5 to 8

GROUND COVERS

Lady's mantle
*Alchemilla
mollis*
Zones 4 to 7

Rockspray
cotoneaster
*Cotoneaster
horizontalis*
Zones 5 to 9

Maiden pink
*Dianthus
deltoides*
Zones 3 to 8

Red
barrenwort
*Epimedium ×
rubrum*
Zones 5 to 8

Wintercreeper
euonymus
*Euonymus
fortunei*
Zones 5 to 8

Lenten rose
*Helleborus
orientalis*
Zones 4 to 9

Evergreen
candytuft
*Iberis
sempervirens*
Zones 5 to 10

Japanese
garden juniper
*Juniperus
procumbens*
Zones 5 to 9

Lamb's-ears
*Stachys
byzantina*
Zones 4 to 7

Allegheny
foamflower
*Tiarella
cordifolia*
Zones 3 to 8

PERENNIALS

Astilbe
Astilbe hybrids
Zones 4 to 8

Japanese
painted fern
*Athyrium
nipponicum*
'Pictum'
Zones 3 to 8

Delphinium
*Delphinium
elatum*
Zones 2 to 7

Bloody
cranesbill
*Geranium
sanguineum*
Zones 3 to 8

Blue oat grass
*Helictotrichon
sempervirens*
Zones 4 to 9

Hosta
Hosta hybrids
Zones 3 to 8

Siberian iris
Iris sibirica
Zones 3 to 9

Shasta daisy
*Leucanthemum
× superbum*
Zones 5 to 9

Purple moor
grass
*Molinia
caerulea*
Zones 4 to 9

Oriental poppy
*Papaver
orientale*
Zones 2 to 7

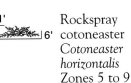

WEST

TREES

20' / 4' Italian cypress
Cupressus sempervirens
Zones 7 to 9

20' / 12' Japanese persimmon
Diospyros kaki
Zone 9

35' / 20' Eucalyptus
Eucalyptus species
Zones 9 to 10

20' / 12' Loquat
Eriobotrya japonica
Zones 8 to 10

20' / 12' Sweet gum
Liquidambar styraciflua
Zones 5 to 10

15' / 15' Olive
Olea europea
Zones 9 to 10

40' / 30' Italian stone pine
Pinus pinea
Zones 8 to 10

15' / 15' Chinese pistachio
Pistacia chinensis
Zones 7 to 9

20' / 20' Coast live oak
Quercus agrifolia
Zone 9

20' / 15' Coast redwood
Sequoia sempervirens
Zones 7 to 9

SHRUBS

3' / 8' California lilac
Ceanothus species
Zones 8 to 10

3' / 4' Rock rose
Cistus species
Zones 8 to 10

3' / 5' Shrubby veronica
Hebe species and hybrids
Zones 8 to 10

10' / 10' New Zealand tea
Leptospermum scoparium
Zones 9 to 10

10' / 6' Myrtle
Myrtus communis
Zones 9 to 10

7' / 4' Heavenly bamboo
Nandina domestica
Zones 7 to 10

5' / 6' Japanese pittosporum
Pittosporum tobira
Zones 8 to 10

15' / 15' Pomegranate
Punica granatum
Zones 8 to 10

4' / 5' Indian hawthorn
Rhaphiolepis indica
Zones 8 to 10

8' / 8' Laurustinus
Viburnum tinus
Zones 8 to 10

GROUND COVERS

20" / 20" African daisy
Arctotis stoechadifolia
Zones 8 to 10

8" / 15" Plumbago
Ceratostigma plumbaginoides
Zones 5 to 9

1' / 6' Rockspray cotoneaster
Cotoneaster horizontalis
Zones 5 to 9

8" / 8" Blue fescue
Festuca glauca
Zones 4 to 9

10" / 9" Gazania
Gazania rigens
Zones 8 to 10

20" / 20" Coral bells
Heuchera hybrids
Zones 3 to 9

1' / 2' Evergreen candytuft
Iberis sempervirens
Zones 5 to 10

2' / 8' Shore juniper
Juniperus conferta
Zones 6 to 10

4' / 6' Rosemary
Rosmarinus officinalis
Zones 7 to 10

1' / 3' Creeping verbena
Verbena hybrids
Zones 6 to 10

PERENNIALS

2' / 2' Yarrow
Achillea hybrids
Zones 3 to 9

3' / 3' Wormwood
Artemisia ludoviciana
Zones 4 to 9

2' / 1' Crocosmia
Crocosmia hybrids
Zones 5 to 9

10" / 12" Twinspur
Diascia hybrids
Zones 8 to 9

7' / 8' Gunnera
Gunnera manicata
Zones 7 to 8

15" / 15" Lenten rose
Helleborus orientalis
Zones 4 to 9

3' / 2' Beard-tongue
Penstemon species and hybrids
Zones 2 to 9

7' / 4' New Zealand flax
Phormium tenax
Zones 8 to 10

2' / 2' Western sword fern
Polystichum munitum
Zones 7 to 9

5' / 3' Giant feather grass
Stipa gigantea
Zones 7 to 10

PACIFIC NORTHWEST

TREES

Paperbark maple
Acer griseum
Zones 5 to 7

Katsura tree
Cercidiphyllum japonicum
Zones 5 to 8

Lawson false cypress
Chamaecyparis lawsoniana
Zones 6 to 8

Japanese cedar
Cryptomeria japonica
Zones 6 to 8

Dove tree
Davidia involucrata
Zones 6 to 8

Star magnolia
Magnolia stellata
Zones 5 to 9

Flowering cherry
Prunus hybrids
Zones 6 to 9

Japanese stewartia
Stewartia pseudocamellia
Zones 6 to 7

Japanese snowbell
Styrax japonica
Zones 6 to 8

American arborvitae
Thuja occidentalis
Zones 4 to 8

SHRUBS

Buttercup winter hazel
Corylopsis pauciflora
Zones 6 to 8

Redvein enkianthus
Enkianthus campanulatus
Zones 5 to 8

Hybrid witch hazel
Hamamelis × intermedia
Zones 5 to 8

Japanese holly
Ilex crenata
Zones 6 to 10

Mountain laurel
Kalmia latifolia
Zones 5 to 8

Oregon grape
Mahonia aquifolium
Zones 5 to 9

Japanese andromeda
Pieris japonica
Zones 6 to 9

Rhododendrons and azaleas
Rhododendron species and hybrids
Zones variable

Roses
Rosa species and hybrids
Zones variable

Yew
Taxus species
Zones 5 to 7

GROUND COVERS

Bearberry
Arctostaphylos uva-ursi
Zones 2 to 8

Bergenia
Bergenia cordifolia
Zones 4 to 8

Scotch heather
Calluna vulgaris
Zones 5 to 8

Bearberry cotoneaster
Cotoneaster dammeri
Zones 5 to 8

Lenten rose
Helleborus orientalis
Zones 4 to 9

Evergreen candytuft
Iberis sempervirens
Zones 5 to 10

Shore juniper
Juniperus conferta
Zones 6 to 10

Creeping phlox
Phlox subulata
Zones 2 to 8

Bethlehem sage
Pulmonaria saccharata
Zones 3 to 8

Allegheny foamflower
Tiarella cordifolia
Zones 3 to 8

PERENNIALS

Maidenhair fern
Adiantum pedatum
Zones 3 to 8

Columbine
Aquilegia hybrids
Zones 3 to 9

Yellow corydalis
Corydalis lutea
Zones 5 to 7

Twinspur
Diascia hybrids
Zones 8 to 9

Japanese golden grass
Hakonechloa macra 'Aureola'
Zones 6 to 7

Japanese primrose
Primula japonica
Zones 5 to 9

Chinese rhubarb
Rheum palmatum
Zones 5 to 7

Rodgersia
Rodgersia pinnata
Zones 5 to 7

Meadow rue
Thalictrum rochebrunianum
Zones 4 to 9

Toad lily
Tricyrtis hirta
Zones 4 to 8

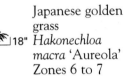

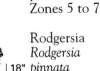
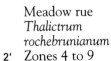

SOUTHWEST

TREES

25'

Box elder
Acer negundo
Zones 2 to 9

10'
Crimson bottlebrush
Callistemon citrinus
Zones 9 to 10

20'
Arizona cypress
Cupressus arizonica
Zones 7 to 9

20'
Loquat
Eriobotrya japonica
Zones 8 to 10

15'
Crape myrtle
Lagerstroemia indica
Zones 7 to 9

15'
Olive
Olea europaea
Zones 9 to 10

15'
Chinese pistachio
Pistacia chinensis
Zones 7 to 9

20'
Pepper tree
Schinus molle
Zones 9 to 10

12'
Five-stamen tamarisk
Tamarix ramosissima
Zones 4 to 8

15'

Chinese date
Ziziphus jujuba
Zones 6 to 9

SHRUBS

6'
Mirror plant
Coprosma repens
Zones 9 to 10

10'
Silverberry
Elaeagnus pungens
Zones 7 to 10

10'
Myrtle
Myrtus communis
Zones 9 to 10

7'
Heavenly bamboo
Nandina domestica
Zones 7 to 10

15'
Oleander
Nerium oleander
Zones 8 to 10

5'
Japanese pittosporum
Pittosporum tobira
Zones 8 to 10

15'
Pomegranate
Punica granatum
Zones 8 to 10

10'
Scarlet firethorn
Pyracantha coccinea
Zones 6 to 9

4'
Indian hawthorn
Rhaphiolepis indica
Zones 8 to 10

6'
Adam's needle
Yucca filamentosa
Zones 5 to 9

GROUND COVERS

20"
African daisy
Arctotis stoechadifolia
Zones 8 to 10

3'
Wormwood
Artemisia ludoviciana
Zones 4 to 9

1'
Rockspray cotoneaster
Cotoneaster horizontalis
Zones 5 to 9

10"
Gazania
Gazania rigens
Zones 8 to 10

8"
Blue fescue
Festuca glauca
Zones 4 to 9

3'
Goldencup St. John's wort
Hypericum × patulum
Zones 7 to 10

1'
Evergreen candytuft
Iberis sempervirens
Zones 5 to 10

6'
San Jose juniper
Juniperus chinensis 'San Jose'
Zones 4 to 10

4'
Rosemary
Rosmarinus officinalis
Zones 7 to 10

1'
Creeping verbena
Verbena hybrids
Zones 6 to 10

PERENNIALS

2'

Yarrow
Achillea hybrids
Zones 3 to 9

2'
Butterfly weed
Asclepias tuberosa
Zones 4 to 9

4'
Feather reed grass
Calamagrostis × acutiflora 'Stricta'
Zones 6 to 9

9"
Blanket flower
Gaillardia × grandiflora
Zones 2 to 9

30"
Blue oat grass
Helictotrichon sempervirens
Zones 4 to 9

30"

Beard-tongue
Penstemon species and hybrids
Zones 2 to 9

4'
Russian sage
Perovskia atriplicifolia
Zones 2 to 9

24"
Stonecrop
Sedum spectabile
Zones 3 to 10

5'

Giant feather grass
Stipa gigantea
Zones 7 to 10

3'

Mullein
Verbascum chaixii
Zones 5 to 8

SOUTHEAST/GULF

TREES

12' 15' Silk tree
*Albizia
julibrissin*
Zones 6 to 9

15' 15' Crape myrtle
*Lagerstroemia
indica*
Zones 7 to 9

25' 20' Southern
magnolia
*Magnolia
grandiflora*
Zones 7 to 9

20' 15' Sweet bay
magnolia
*Magnolia
virginiana*
Zones 5 to 9

20' 15' Black gum
Nyssa sylvatica
Zones 5 to 9

30' 30' Empress tree
*Paulownia
tomentosa*
Zones 7 to 9

20' 20' Southern live
oak
*Quercus
virginiana*
Zone 9

25' 15' Chinese tallow
tree
*Sapium
sebiferum*
Zones 8 to 10

30' 15' Bald cypress
*Taxodium
distichum*
Zones 3 to 10

20' 20' Chaste tree
*Vitex
agnus-castus*
Zones 7 to 9

SHRUBS

6' 5' Japanese
aucuba
*Aucuba
japonica*
Zones 7 to 10

8' 8' Carolina
allspice
*Calycanthus
floridus*
Zones 5 to 9

10' 6' Camellia
*Camellia
japonica*
Zones 8 to 10

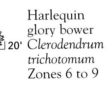
15' 20' Harlequin
glory bower
*Clerodendrum
trichotomum*
Zones 6 to 9

3' 3' Winter daphne
Daphne odora
Zones 8 to 10

10' 15' Silverberry
*Elaeagnus
pungens*
Zones 7 to 10

6' 6' Gardenia
*Gardenia
jasminoides*
Zones 8 to 10

7' 6' Leatherleaf
mahonia
Mahonia bealei
Zones 6 to 10

15' 10' Sweet olive
*Osmanthus
fragrans*
Zones 8 to 10

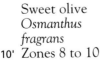
8' 10' Roses
Rosa species
and hybrids
Zones variable

GROUND COVERS

8' 15" Variegated
Japanese sedge
Carex morrowii
'Variegata'
Zones 5 to 9

2' 2' Daylily
Hemerocallis,
evergreen
hybrids
Zones 6 to 10

3' 4' Goldencup
St. John's wort
Hypericum ×
patulum
Zones 7 to 10

1' 2' Evergreen
candytuft
*Iberis
sempervirens*
Zones 5 to 10

12" 10" Impatiens
Impatiens
hybrids
Annual

2' 8' Shore juniper
*Juniperus
conferta*
Zones 6 to 10

6" 6" Ice plant
*Mesembryan-
themum*
Annual

10" 18" Chilean
bellflower
*Nolana
paradoxa*
Zones 8 to 10

4" 12" Swedish ivy
Plectranthus
Zones 9 to 10

4' 6' Rosemary
*Rosmarinus
officinalis*
Zones 7 to 10

PERENNIALS

2' 2' Butterfly weed
*Asclepias
tuberosa*
Zones 4 to 9

2' 2' Threadleaf
coreopsis
*Coreopsis
verticillata*
Zones 5 to 9

7' 5' Pampas grass
*Cortaderia
selloana*
Zones 6 to 9

9" 12" Blanket flower
Gaillardia ×
grandiflora
Zones 2 to 9

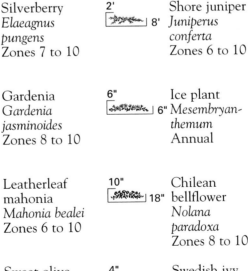
5' 3' Rose mallow
*Hibiscus
moscheutos*
Zones 5 to 9

5' 4' Tree mallow
*Lavatera
thuringiaca*
Zones 6 to 9

8' 3' Maiden grass
*Miscanthus
sinensis*
Zones 6 to 9

7' 4' New Zealand
flax
Phormium tenax
Zones 8 to 10

24" 18" Stonecrop
*Sedum
spectabile*
Zones 3 to 10

6' 3' Yucca
*Yucca
filamentosa*
Zones 4 to 10

SOUTHEAST/MID-ATLANTIC

TREES

Pawpaw
Asimina triloba
Zones 5 to 8

River birch
Betula nigra
Zones 4 to 9

White fringe tree
Chionanthus virginicus
Zones 5 to 9

Yellowwood
Cledratis lutea
Zones 5 to 8

Sweet gum
Liquidambar styraciflua
Zones 5 to 10

Tulip tree
Liriodendron tulipifera
Zones 5 to 9

Bigleaf magnolia
Magnolia macrophylla
Zones 5 to 9

Chinese quince
Pseudocydonia sinensis
Zones 6 to 9

Willow oak
Quercus phellos
Zones 6 to 9

Chinese elm
Ulmus parvifolia
Zones 6 to 9

SHRUBS

Glossy abelia
Abelia × grandiflora
Zones 6 to 9

Butterfly bush
Buddleia davidii
Zones 5 to 9

Common boxwood
Buxus sempervirens
Zones 6 to 10

Summersweet
Clethra alnifolia
Zones 3 to 9

Rose of Sharon
Hibiscus syriacus
Zones 5 to 9

Bigleaf Hydrangea
Hydrangea macrophylla
Zones 7 to 10

Oakleaf hydrangea
Hydrangea quercifolia
Zones 5 to 8

Chinese holly
Ilex cornuta
Zones 7 to 9

Scarlet firethorn
Pyracantha coccinea
Zones 6 to 9

Rhododendrons and azaleas
Rhododendron species and hybrids
Zones variable

GROUND COVERS

Wormwood
Artemisia ludovisiana
Zones 4 to 9

Bergenia
Bergenia cordifolia
Zones 4 to 9

Plumbago
Ceratostigma plumbaginoides
Zones 5 to 9

Hay-scented fern
Dennstaedtia punctiloba
Zones 3 to 8

Red barrenwort
Epimedium × rubrum
Zones 5 to 8

Winter creeper euonymus
Euonymus fortunei
Zones 5 to 8

Mediterranean spurge
Euphorbia characias
Zones 7 to 9

Lenten rose
Helleborus orientalis
Zones 4 to 9

Creeping juniper
Juniperus horizontalis
Zones 3 to 9

Sage
Salvia × sylvestris
Zones 4 to 8

PERENNIALS

Yarrow
Achillea hybrids
Zones 3 to 9

Hardy aster
Aster species and hybrids
Zones 4 to 9

Feather reed grass
Calamagrostis × acutiflora 'Stricta'
Zones 6 to 9

Crocosmia
Crocosmia hybrids
Zones 5 to 8

Blanket flower
Gaillardia × grandiflora
Zones 2 to 9

Blue oat grass
Helictotrichon sempervirens
Zones 4 to 9

Bearded iris
Iris hybrids
Zones 3 to 10

Cardinal flower
Lobelia cardinalis
Zones 2 to 9

Stokes' aster
Stokesia laevis
Zones 5 to 9

Yucca
Yucca filamentosa
Zones 4 to 10

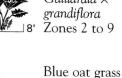
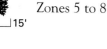

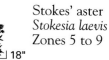

MOUNTAIN

TREES

15' · 10'
White fir
Abies concolor
Zones 4 to 8

10' · 8'
Amur maple
Acer ginnala
Zones 3 to 8

25' · 12'
European
white birch
Betula pendula
Zones 3 to 6

20' · 20'
Russian olive
*Elaeagnus
angustifolia*
Zones 3 to 7

15' · 15'
Crabapple
Malus hybrids
Zones 4 to 8

15' · 6'
Colorado blue
spruce
*Picea pungens
glauca*
Zones 3 to 7

25' · 8'
Quaking aspen
*Populus
tremuloides*
Zones 2 to 6

20' · 20'
Amur cherry
Prunus maackii
Zones 3 to 6

20' · 15'
European
mountain ash
*Sorbus
aucuparia*
Zones 3 to 6

20' · 10'
Littleleaf
linden
Tilia cordata
Zones 4 to 3

SHRUBS

20' · 15'
Siberian pea
shrub
*Caragana
arborescens*
Zones 2 to 7

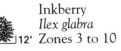
10' · 15'
Redtwig
dogwood
Cornus alba
'Sibirica'
Zones 3 to 8

8' · 12'
Inkberry
Ilex glabra
Zones 3 to 10

4' · 8'
Rocky
Mountain
juniper
*Juniperus
scopulorum*
Zones 4 to 8

8' · 8'
Northern
bayberry
*Myrica
pensylvanica*
Zones 2 to 7

3' · 6'
Bird's-nest
spruce
Picea abies
'Nidiformis'
Zones 2 to 5

16' · 20'
Mugo pine
*Pinus mugo
mugo*
Zones 2 to 8

3' · 3'
Bush-
cinquefoil
*Potentilla
fruticosa*
Zones 3 to 7

15' · 15'
Nanking
cherry
*Prunus
tomentosa*
Zones 2 to 7

6' · 5'
Alpine currant
Ribes alpinum
Zones 2 to 7

GROUND COVERS

1' · 5'
Bearberry
*Arctostaphylos
uva-ursi*
Zones 2 to 7

9" · 12"
Basket-of-gold
*Aurinia
saxatilis*
Zones 3 to 7

10" · 18"
Maiden Pink
*Dianthus
deltoides*
Zones 3 to 8

12" · 18"
Bloody
cranesbill
*Geranium
sanguineum*
Zones 3 to 8

20" · 20"
Coral bells
Heuchera
hybrids
Zones 3 to 8

6" · 12"
Dwarf
crested iris
Iris cristata
Zones 3 to 8

10' · 12'
Mountain
juniper
*Juniperus
communis
alpina*
Zones 3 to 7

6" · 4'
Creeping
juniper
*Juniperus
horizontalis*
Zones 3 to 9

6" · 12"
Creeping
phlox
Phlox subulata
Zones 2 to 8

12" · 12"
Lamb's ears
*Stachys
byzantina*
Zones 4 to 7

PERENNIALS

3' · 1'
Monkshood
Aconitum
species and
hybrids
Zones 3 to 7

2' · 1'
Columbine
Aquilegia
species and
hybrids
Zones 3 to 9

5' · 3'
Delphinium
*Delphinium
elatum*
Zones 2 to 7

30" · 18"
Bleeding heart
Dicentra eximia
and hybrids
Zones 2 to 8

3' · 3'
Baby's breath
*Gypsophila
paniculata*
Zones 3 to 7

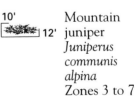
3' · 2'
Siberian iris
Iris sibirica
Zones 3 to 9

5' · 3'
Ostrich fern
*Matteuccia
struthiopteris*
Zones 2 to 7

5' · 2'
Switch grass
*Panicum
virgatum*
Zones 3 to 9

3' · 2'
Oriental poppy
*Papaver
orientale*
Zones 2 to 7

30" · 18"
Beard-tongue
Penstemon
species and
hybrids
Zones 2 to 9

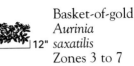

THE USDA PLANT HARDINESS ZONE MAP OF NORTH AMERICA

Plants are classified according to the amount of cold weather they can handle. For example, a plant listed as hardy to zone 6 will survive a winter in which the temperature drops to minus 10° F.

Warm weather also influences whether a plant will survive in your region. Although this map does not address heat hardiness, in general, if a range of hardiness zones are listed for a plant, the plant will survive winter in the coldest zone as well as tolerate the heat of the warmest zone.

To use this map, find the location of your community, then match the color band marking that area to the zone key at left.

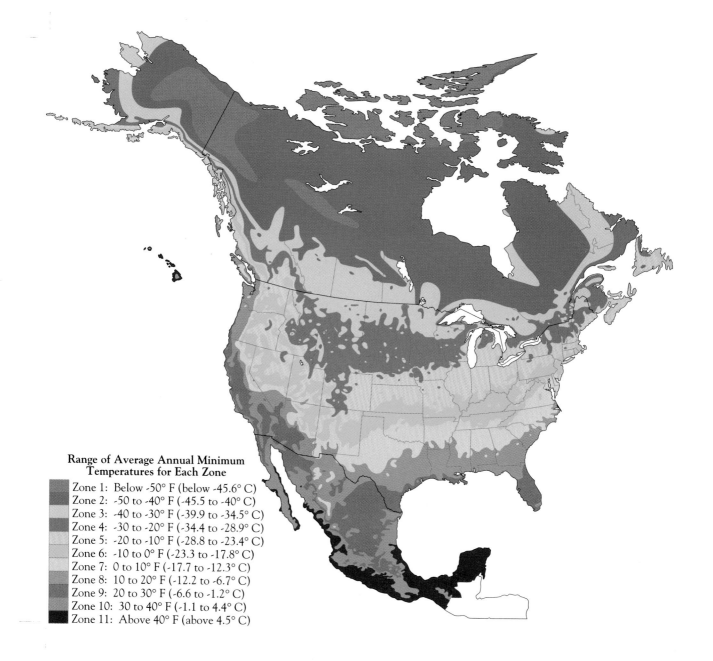

Range of Average Annual Minimum Temperatures for Each Zone

Zone 1: Below -50° F (below -45.6° C)
Zone 2: -50 to -40° F (-45.5 to -40° C)
Zone 3: -40 to -30° F (-39.9 to -34.5° C)
Zone 4: -30 to -20° F (-34.4 to -28.9° C)
Zone 5: -20 to -10° F (-28.8 to -23.4° C)
Zone 6: -10 to 0° F (-23.3 to -17.8° C)
Zone 7: 0 to 10° F (-17.7 to -12.3° C)
Zone 8: 10 to 20° F (-12.2 to -6.7° C)
Zone 9: 20 to 30° F (-6.6 to -1.2° C)
Zone 10: 30 to 40° F (-1.1 to 4.4° C)
Zone 11: Above 40° F (above 4.5° C)

INDEX

Page numbers in italics denote photographs and plans.

METRIC CONVERSIONS

U.S. Units to Metric Equivalents			Metric Units to U.S. Equivalents		
To Convert From	**Multiply By**	**To Get**	**To Convert From**	**Multiply By**	**To Get**
Inches	25.4	Millimeters	Millimeters	0.0394	Inches
Inches	2.54	Centimeters	Centimeters	0.3937	Inches
Feet	30.48	Centimeters	Centimeters	0.0328	Feet
Feet	0.3048	Meters	Meters	3.2808	Feet
Yards	0.9144	Meters	Meters	1.0936	Yards
Square inches	6.4516	Square centimeters	Square centimeters	0.1550	Square inches
Square feet	0.0929	Square meters	Square meters	10.764	Square feet
Square yards	0.8361	Square meters	Square meters	1.1960	Square yards
Acres	0.4047	Hectares	Hectares	2.4711	Acres
Cubic inches	16.387	Cubic centimeters	Cubic centimeters	0.0610	Cubic inches
Cubic feet	0.0283	Cubic meters	Cubic meters	35.315	Cubic feet
Cubic feet	28.316	Liters	Liters	0.0353	Cubic feet
Cubic yards	0.7646	Cubic meters	Cubic meters	1.308	Cubic yards
Cubic yards	764.55	Liters	Liters	0.0013	Cubic yards

To convert from degrees Fahrenheit (F) to degrees Celsius (C), first subtract 32, then multiply by ⁵⁄₉.

To convert from degrees Celsius to degrees Fahrenheit, multiply by ⁹⁄₅, then add 32.